OFFICIAL PAST PAPERS WITH ANSWERS

INTERMEDIATE 2

# GEOGRAPHY
## 2007-2011

## Publisher's Note

We are delighted to bring you the 2011 Past Papers and you will see that we have changed the format from previous editions. As part of our environmental awareness strategy, we have attempted to make these new editions as sustainable as possible.

To do this, we have printed on white paper and bound the answer sections into the book. This not only allows us to use significantly less paper but we are also, for the first time, able to source all the materials from sustainable sources.

We hope you like the new editions and by purchasing this product, you are not only supporting an independent Scottish publishing company but you are also, in the International Year of Forests, not contributing to the destruction of the world's forests.

Thank you for your support and please see the following websites for more information to support the above statement –

www.fsc-uk.org

www.loveforests.com

© Scottish Qualifications Authority
All rights reserved. Copying prohibited. No part of this publication may be reproduced, stored in a retrieval system, or transmitted in any form or by any means, electronic, mechanical, photocopying, recording or otherwise.

First exam published in 2007.
Published by Bright Red Publishing Ltd, 6 Stafford Street, Edinburgh EH3 7AU
tel: 0131 220 5804 fax: 0131 220 6710 info@brightredpublishing.co.uk  www.brightredpublishing.co.uk

ISBN 978-1-84948-199-1

A CIP Catalogue record for this book is available from the British Library.

Bright Red Publishing is grateful to the copyright holders, as credited on the final page of the Question Section, for permission to use their material. Every effort has been made to trace the copyright holders and to obtain their permission for the use of copyright material.
Bright Red Publishing will be happy to receive information allowing us to rectify any error or omission in future editions.

[BLANK PAGE]

# X208/201

NATIONAL
QUALIFICATIONS
2007

MONDAY, 28 MAY
9.00 AM – 11.00 AM

GEOGRAPHY
INTERMEDIATE 2

Candidates should answer **four** questions:

Section A    Question 1
**and**
Question 2

**AND**

Section B    any **two** questions from
Questions 3 to 7

Candidates should read the questions carefully.    Answers should be clearly expressed and relevant.

Credit will always be given for appropriate sketch-maps and diagrams.

Write legibly and neatly, and leave a space of about one cm between the lines.

All maps and diagrams in this paper have been printed in black only:  no other colours have been used.

SCOTTISH
QUALIFICATIONS
AUTHORITY
©

1:50 000 Scale
Landranger Series

Scale 1: 50 000
2 centimetres to 1 kilometre (one grid square)

2   1   0   Kilometres   1   2   3

1   0   Miles   1   2

1 kilometre = 0·6214 mile         1 mile = 1·6093 kilometres

Magnetic North   Grid North   True North

Diagrammatic only

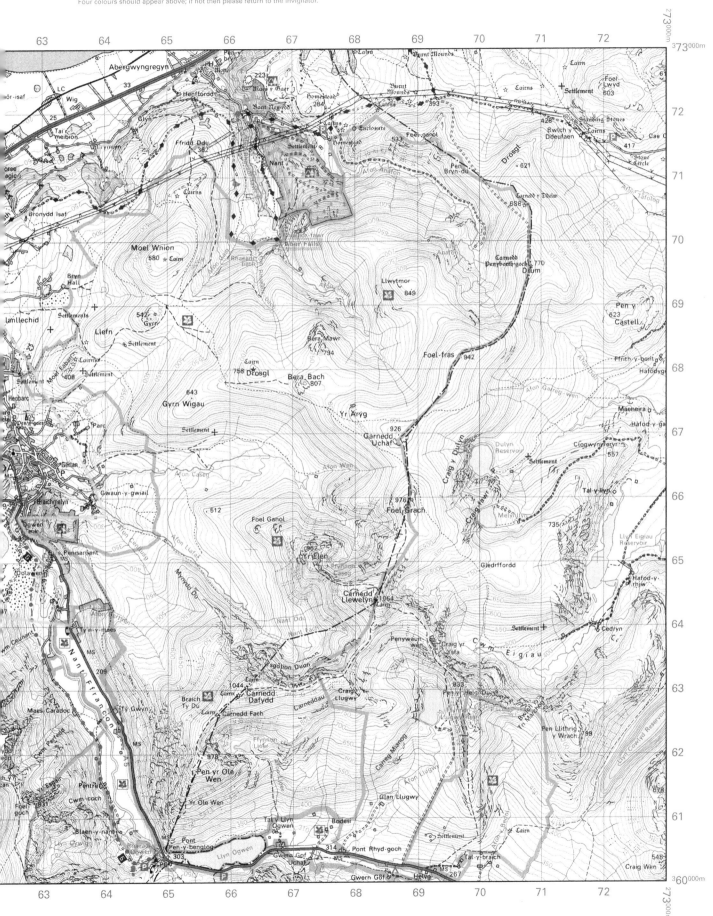

*Mark*

## SECTION A

### IN THIS SECTION YOU <u>MUST</u> ANSWER QUESTION 1 <u>AND</u> QUESTION 2.

**Question 1: Physical Environments**

Study the Ordnance Survey Map Extract No 1559/115.

(*a*) Describe the **physical** features of the river Afon Ogwen **and** its valley from grid reference 650604 to grid reference 611722.      **4**

(*b*) **Identify** the feature of glacial erosion found at each of the grid references below.

         662622          645610          673653          660605

Choose from:

         Corrie      Pyramidal Peak      Ribbon Lake      U-shaped Valley.      **3**

(*c*) **Explain** how a corrie is formed.

You may use a diagram(s) to illustrate your answer.      **4**

*Marks*

1. **(continued)**

### Reference Diagram Q1A: Selected Land Uses in National Parks

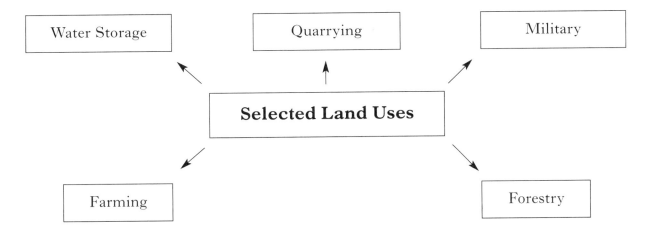

### Reference Diagram Q1B: Aims of National Parks

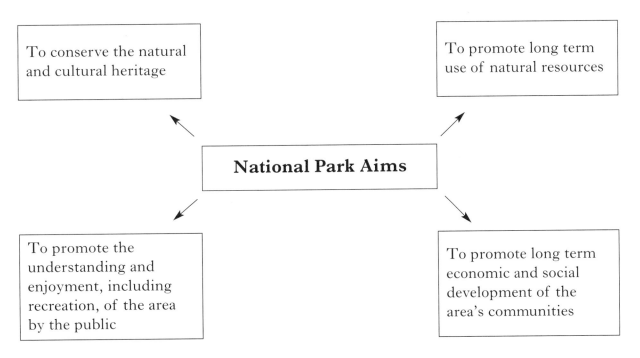

(*d*) Look at Reference Diagrams Q1A and Q1B.

Select **two** land uses from Reference Diagram Q1A.

**Explain**, in detail, different ways in which your chosen land uses are in conflict with the aims of the National Parks.     5

(*e*) (i) For a coastal area you have studied, **explain**, in detail, the benefits and problems which tourism has brought to the area.     5

     (ii) Describe, in detail, ways in which public **and** voluntary organisations attempt to manage problems caused by tourism in such areas.     4

          **(25)**

*[END OF QUESTION 1]*

**NOW GO ON TO QUESTION 2**

*Mark*

### Question 2: Human Environments

**Reference Diagram Q2A:  Projected Changes in Urban/Rural Population for Economically Less Developed Countries**

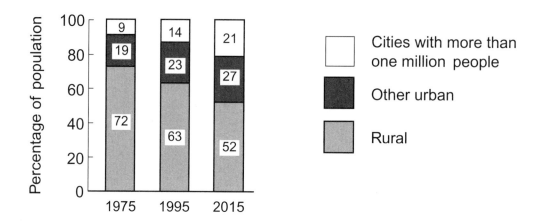

(*a*)  Study Reference Diagram Q2A.

    (i)   Describe, in detail, the trends shown from 1975 to 2015.    **3**

    (ii)  **Explain** the changes shown for cities with more than one million people.    **4**

**Reference Diagram Q2B:  Population Pyramid for Canada in 2008**

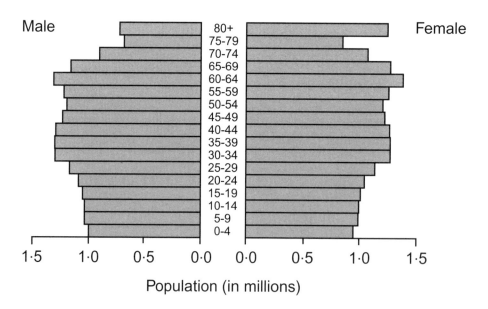

(*b*)  Study Reference Diagram Q2B.

    For Canada, or any other EMDC* you have studied, describe the long term problems which may be caused by its population structure.    **5**

\*EMDC = *economically more developed country*

2. **(continued)**

**Reference Diagram Q2C: Shopping Area, Cardiff City Centre**

(c) Study Reference Diagram Q2C.

For a named city you have studied in an EMDC, give reasons for the main changes which have taken place in the city centre shopping area over the last thirty years.    **5**

**Reference Diagram Q2D: European Agricultural Policies**

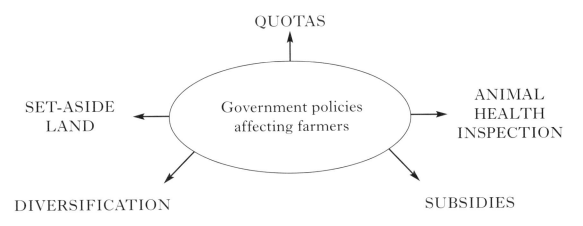

(d) Study Reference Diagram Q2D.

For **two** of the policies shown above, **explain** why they were necessary.    **4**

**[Turn over**

*Mark*

2.    **(continued)**

**Reference Diagram Q2E:  Bangor Industrial Estate**

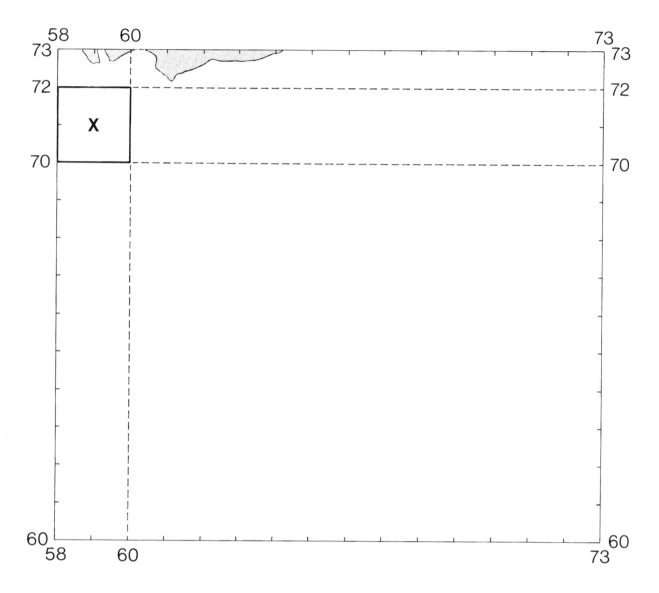

(e)  Study the Ordnance Survey Map Extract No 1559/115 and Reference Diagram Q2E.

Bangor industrial estate is located in area X.

Using map evidence, discuss the suitability of this site for an industrial estate.    **4**

**(25)**

*[END OF SECTION A]*

**NOW TURN TO SECTION B AND ANSWER TWO QUESTIONS**

[BLANK PAGE]

## SECTION B

**Environmental Interactions**

**Answer any two questions from this section.**

Choose from

**SECTION B**

*Marks*

**Question 3: Rural Land Degradation**

**Reference Map Q3A: Distribution of Original and Remaining Forests**

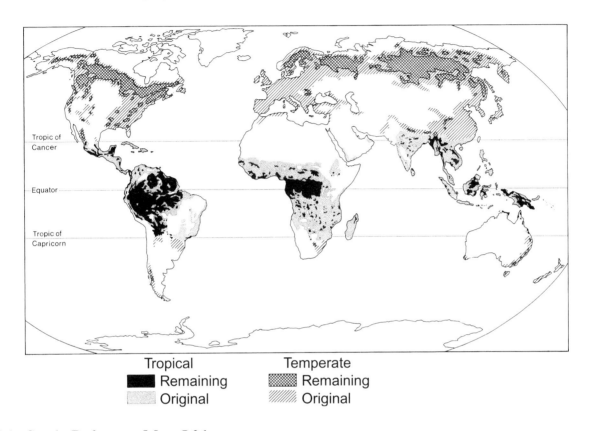

Tropical
■ Remaining
▨ Original

Temperate
▨ Remaining
▨ Original

(*a*)  Study Reference Map Q3A.

For a forest area you have studied:

   (i)   **explain** the impact of increasing population density on the rate of deforestation;   **5**

   (ii)  describe ways in which the rate of deforestation can be reduced.   **4**

**Reference Diagram Q3B: World Desertification**

30% of the
earth's land
surface is affected
by the degradation
of fragile
drylands

(*b*)  Study Reference Diagram Q3B.

Describe the effects of continuing desertification on the human **and** physical environment of arid or semi-arid areas you have studied.   **6**

**(15)**

*Mark*

**Question 4:  River Basin Management**

**Reference Diagram Q4A:  Factors affecting Water Movement and Storage in a River Basin**

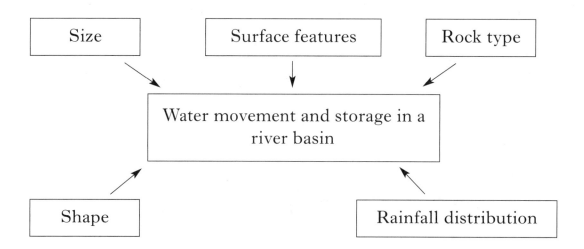

(*a*)  For any river basin you have studied, **explain** how the factors shown above can affect the movement and storage of water.    **6**

*Marks*

**4.  (continued)**

**Reference Diagram Q4B:  The Hydrological Cycle**

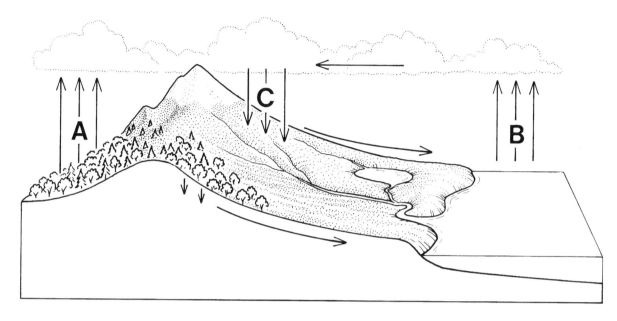

(b)  Look at Reference Diagram Q4B.

Describe, in detail, the processes taking place at A, B and C.          **4**

**[Turn over**

*Mark*

4.   **(continued)**

Reference Map Q4C:  Columbia River Basin Water Management

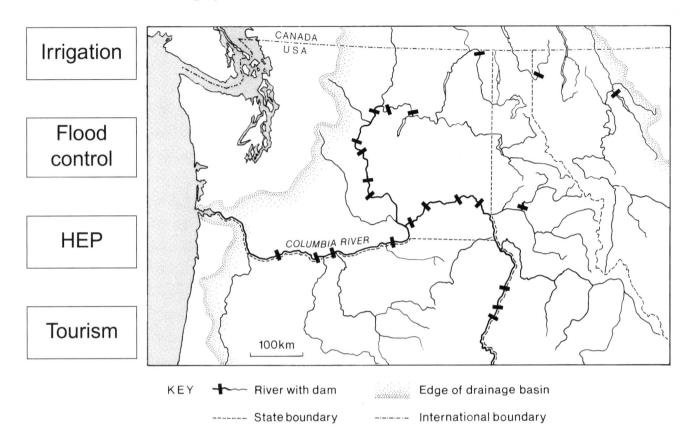

(c)   Study Reference Map Q4C.

For this river basin, or any other you have studied, **explain** the benefits which a river basin management project can bring to the people and environment of the area.    **5**

**(15)**

*Marks*

**Question 5:  European Environmental Inequalities**

**Reference Map Q5A:  Pattern of Acid Rain in Europe**

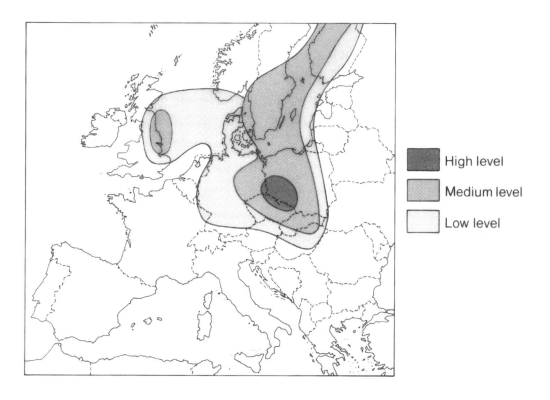

Study Reference Map Q5A.

(*a*)  (i)   Describe the variations in levels of acid rain throughout Europe.    **3**

(ii)  **Explain** how economic activity **and** climate affect levels of acid rain throughout Europe.    **4**

**[Turn over**

*Mar*

**5.　(continued)**

### Reference Diagrams Q5B(i):　Coastal Areas

Magaluf

Camargue

### Reference Diagrams Q5B(ii):　Mountain Areas

Zermatt

North West Highlands

(*b*)　Study the photos above.

　　　Reference Diagram Q5B(i) shows two sea/coastal areas.

　　　Reference Diagram Q5B(ii) shows two mountain areas.

　　　For **either** two sea/coastal areas **or** two mountain areas in Europe you have studied, **explain** the differences in their environmental quality.

　　　You may use the examples shown if you wish.　　　　　　　　　　　　　　**4**

(*c*)　Giving examples, describe ways in which countries and people have co-operated to improve the quality of European rivers.　　　　　　　　**4**

**(15)**

*Marks*

## Question 6: Development and Health

Levels of development within a country can be measured using either social or economic indicators.

(*a*) Explain why using one social **or** one economic indicator may not show a country's level of development.

5

### Reference Map Q6: Worldwide Malaria Distribution in 2002

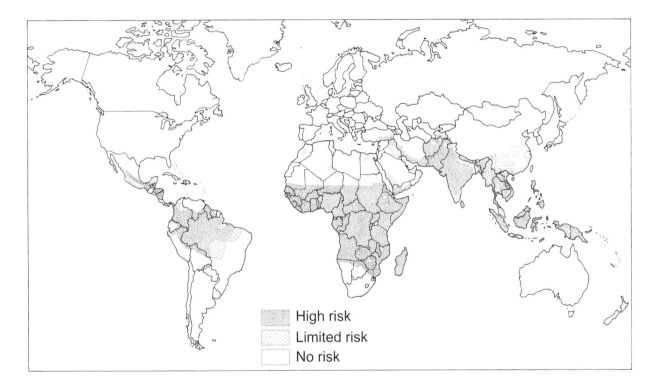

High risk
Limited risk
No risk

(*b*) Study Reference Map Q6.

Referring to the map, describe the distribution of malaria throughout the world.

3

(*c*)  (i) For **either** AIDS, Malaria **or** Heart Disease, describe some of the methods used to control the disease.

4

   (ii) How effective have these methods been?

3

**(15)**

**[Turn over**

*Mark*

### Question 7:  Environmental Hazards

### Reference Map Q7A:  Tropical Storms

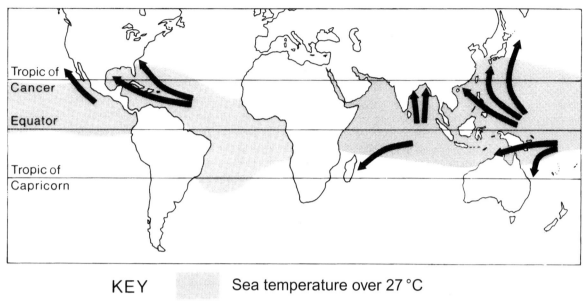

KEY    Sea temperature over 27 °C

Tropical storm routes

(a)  Study Reference Map Q7A.

Using the information shown on the map, **explain**, in detail, the distribution of tropical storms throughout the world.    **4**

*Marks*

**7.    (continued)**

**Reference Diagram Q7B:  Boxing Day Tsunami 2004—Indian Ocean**

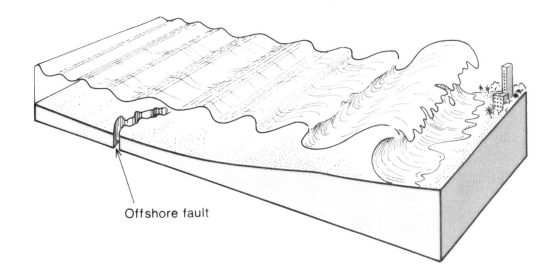

Offshore fault

(*b*)  Study Reference Diagram Q7B.

> The Boxing Day tsunami was caused by a massive underwater earthquake.

(i)   Describe the effects of this, **or any other earthquake**, on the people and
surrounding areas.                                                                          **4**

(ii)  For your chosen earthquake, describe the role of aid agencies involved in the
rescue operations.                                                                          **4**

(iii) How effective were their efforts?                                                     **3**

**(15)**

*[END OF QUESTION PAPER]*

[BLANK PAGE]

# 2008

[BLANK PAGE]

# X208/201

NATIONAL
QUALIFICATIONS
2008

THURSDAY, 22 MAY
9.00 AM – 11.00 AM

GEOGRAPHY
INTERMEDIATE 2

Candidates should answer **four** questions:

| | | |
|---|---|---|
| | Section A | Question 1 **and** Question 2 |
| **AND** | | |
| | Section B | any **two** questions from Questions 3 to 7 |

Candidates should read the questions carefully. Answers should be clearly expressed and relevant.

Credit will always be given for appropriate sketch-maps and diagrams.

Write legibly and neatly, and leave a space of about one cm between the lines.

All maps and diagrams in this paper have been printed in black only: no other colours have been used.

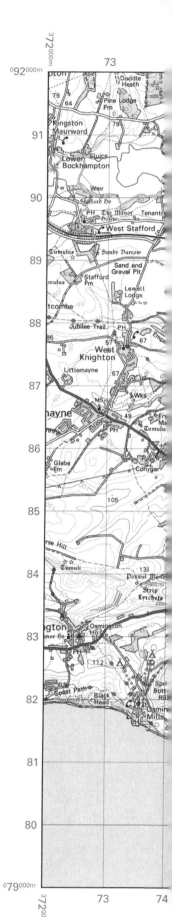

1:50 000 Scale
Landranger Series

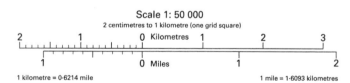

Scale 1: 50 000
2 centimetres to 1 kilometre (one grid square)

1 kilometre = 0·6214 mile          1 mile = 1·6093 kilometres

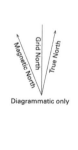

Diagrammatic only

Extract No 1658/194

Four colours should appear above; if not then please return to the invigilator.
Four colours should appear above; if not then please return to the invigilator.

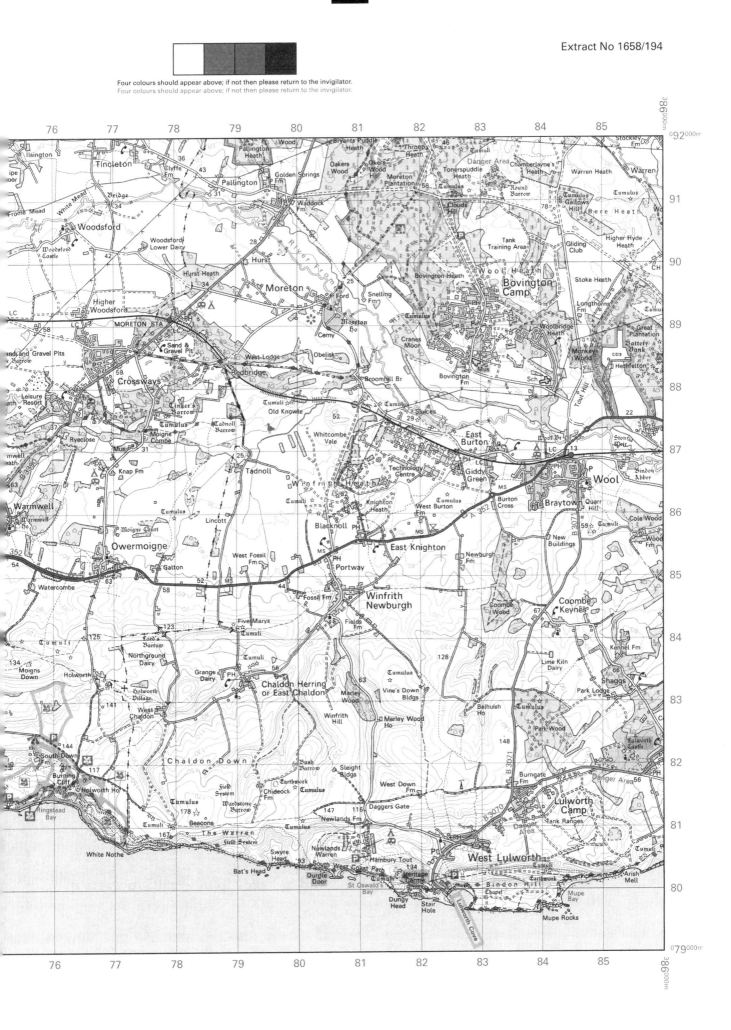

*Mark*

## SECTION A

## IN THIS SECTION YOU <u>MUST</u> ANSWER QUESTION 1 <u>AND</u> QUESTION 2.

**Question 1: Physical Environments**

### Reference Diagram Q1A:  Lulworth/Wool

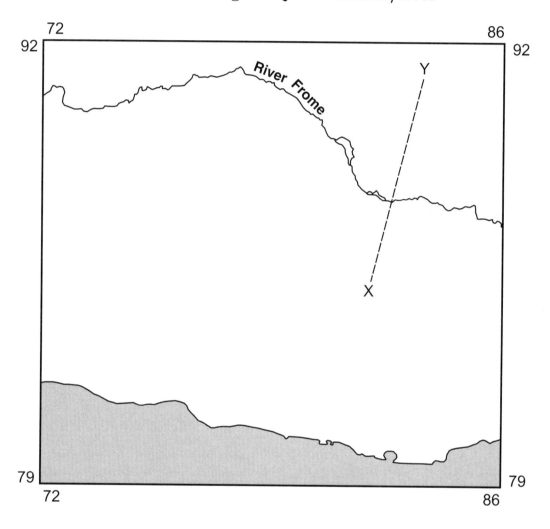

(a) Study the Ordnance Survey Map Extract No 1658/194 of the Lulworth/Wool area and Reference Diagram Q1A.

(i) Choose **either** the physical coastal feature shown in 8279 **or** the physical coastal feature shown in 7780 and explain its formation in detail.

You may wish to use diagrams in your answer.                                       4

(ii) Describe the course of the River Frome **and** its valley from 795905 to where it leaves the map at 860867.                                       4

*Marks*

1.  **(continued)**

### Reference Diagram Q1B:  Land Use Transect X–Y

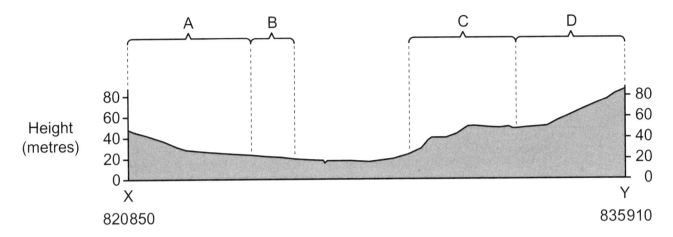

(b)  Study the Ordnance Survey Map of Wool **and** Reference Diagram Q1B.

(i)  Match the letters shown on the transect X–Y above to the land uses listed below.

Land uses:   Industry;    Military Training;    Farmland;    Settlement.    **3**

(ii)  To what extent do you agree that military training activities may be in conflict with other land uses in the area of the map extract?

Give reasons to support your answer.    **4**

**[Turn over**

*Mark*

1. **(continued)**

**Reference Diagram Q1C: Highland Landscape**

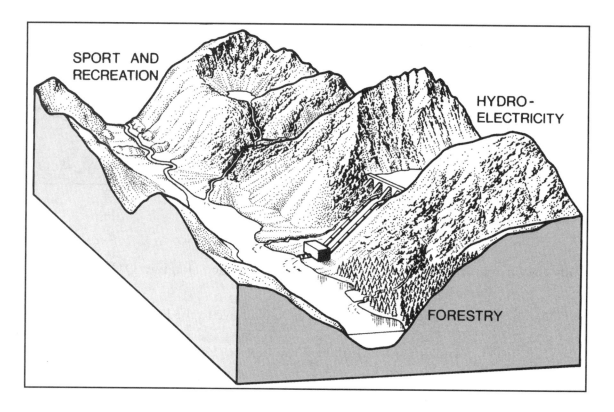

(*c*) Study Reference Diagram Q1C.

  (i) For **one** of the land uses shown, **explain** its economic **and** environmental impact.    **6**

  (ii) Describe strategies which have been used to protect upland environments.    **4**

                                                                **(25)**

*[END OF QUESTION 1]*

**NOW GO ON TO QUESTION 2**

## Question 2:  Human Environments

### Reference Diagram Q2A:  World Population Density

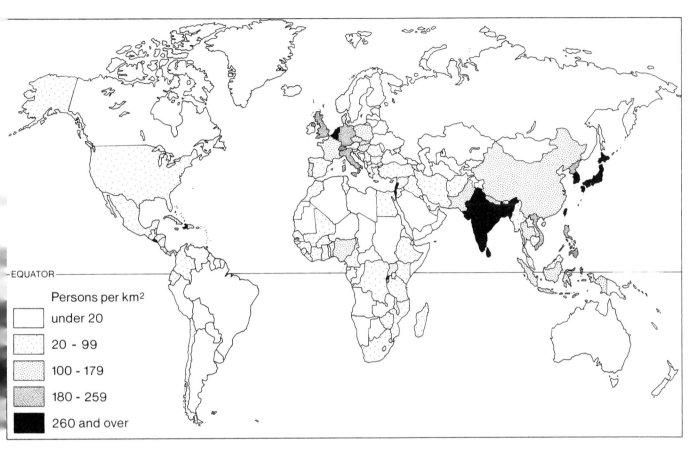

*Marks*

(a)  Study Reference Diagram Q2A.

Referring to both physical **and** human factors, **explain** why some areas of the world have a population density of less than 20 persons per square km.     **5**

**[Turn over**

2.  **(continued)**

**Reference Diagram Q2B:  Birth Rates and Life Expectancy**

|  | Birth Rate/000 | Life Expectancy |
|---|---|---|
| Kenya (K) | 29 | 47 |
| **India (I)** | **24** | **63** |
| Japan (J) | 10 | 81 |
| **Mexico (M)** | **23** | **72** |
| Canada (C) | 11 | 80 |
| **Nigeria (N)** | **40** | **51** |
| Brazil (B) | 18 | 63 |
| **Australia (A)** | **13** | **80** |

(*b*)  Study Reference Diagram Q2B.

(i)  Using the data provided in Reference Diagram Q2B, complete the **scattergraph** by plotting the figures for India, Mexico, Nigeria and Australia on **separate Worksheet Q2(*b*)(i)**.    **2**

(ii)  Describe **and** explain the relationship between Birth Rate and Life Expectancy.    **4**

**Reference Diagram Q2C:  Population Pyramid for Bangladesh, 2005**

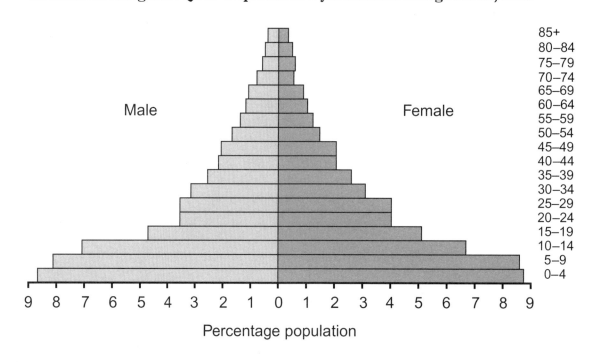

(*c*)  Study Reference Diagram Q2C.

What measures could countries, such as Bangladesh, take to reduce their birth rates?    **4**

*Marks*

## 2. (continued)

**Reference Diagram Q2D:  A Brazilian shanty town**

ELDC  =  Economically less Developed Country
EMDC  =  Economically More Developed Country

(d) For a named **ELDC** city you have studied, describe attempts made to improve living conditions in shanty towns.

5

(e)   *"During recent years the populations of many **EMDC** cities have decreased dramatically due to out-migration."*

Describe ways in which city authorities have attempted to encourage people to **move back** into their city.

5

**(25)**

[*END OF SECTION A*]

**NOW TURN TO SECTION B AND ANSWER TWO QUESTIONS**

**[BLANK PAGE]**

## SECTION B

**Environmental Interactions**

**Answer any two questions from this section.**

Choose from

**[Turn over**

**SECTION B**

*Mark*

## Question 3: Rural Land Degradation

### Reference Diagram Q3A: Logging in Malaysia

(*a*) Study Reference Diagram Q3A.

   (i) Describe the **economic** advantages of increased deforestation. **3**

   (ii) **Explain** ways in which deforestation affects both people **and** the environment. **4**

*Marks*

3. **(continued)**

Reference Diagram Q3B: **Desertification in Australia**

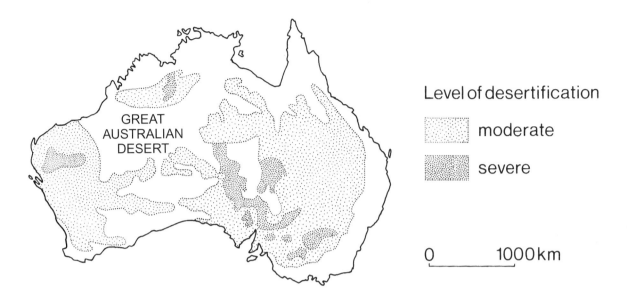

(b) Study Reference Diagram Q3B.

(i) **Explain** the physical **or** human causes of desertification. 4

(ii) For an arid or semi-arid area you have studied, describe methods used to reduce the desertification process. 4

(15)

**[Turn over**

*Marks*

## Question 4:  River Basin Management

**Reference Diagram Q4A:  The Mepanda Uncua Hydropower Project, Mozambique**

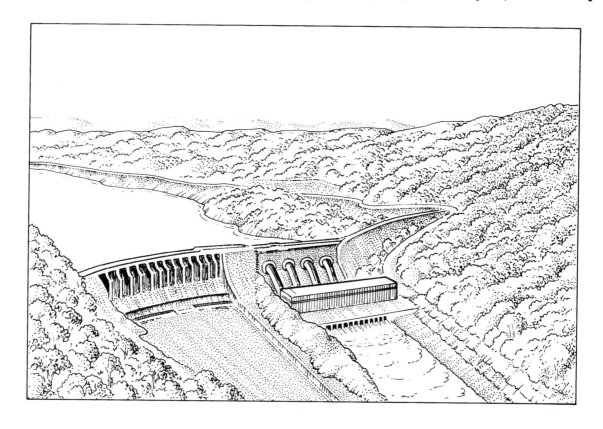

(a)  (i)  Study Reference Diagram Q4A.

For this, or any other river basin project you have studied, describe the **physical** factors which could have influenced the location of the dam.    **4**

(ii)

> ## "Local Community wants proposals for new dam stopped"

Why do some people object to the building of new dams?    **4**

**4.    (continued)**

### Reference Diagram Q4B:
### Proposed Okavango Water Pipeline

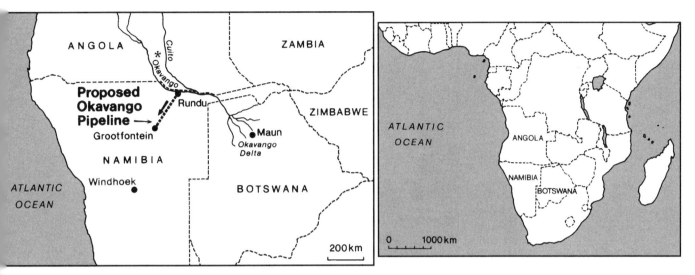

**Note:** * The River Okavango flows from Angola to Botswana

### Reference Diagram Q4C:
### Climate Graph—Grootfontein

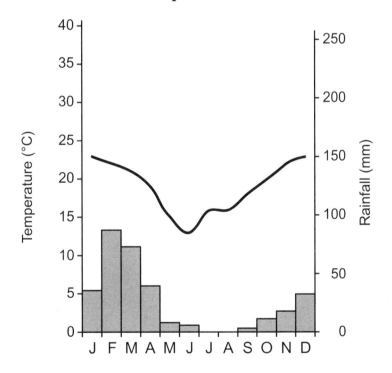

*Marks*

Study Reference Diagrams Q4B and Q4C.

(*b*)  (i)  What benefits could projects such as the proposed Okavango Pipeline bring to
Namibia or similar areas?                                                                                          **4**

(ii)  **Explain** why this pipeline might be a source of conflict between Namibia and
Botswana.                                                                                                                **3**

**(15)**

*Mar*

### Question 5: European Environmental Inequalities

**Reference Map Q5A: Sulphur Dioxide (SO$_2$) Emissions in Europe**

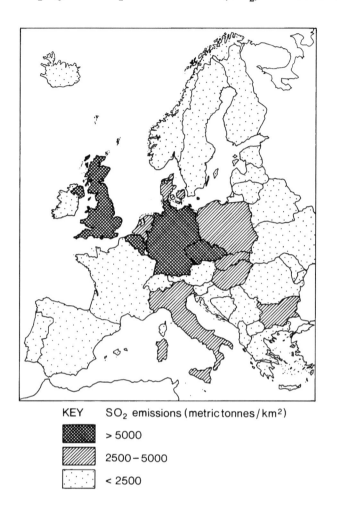

KEY    SO$_2$ emissions (metric tonnes / km$^2$)

> 5000

2500 – 5000

< 2500

(*a*) Study Reference Map Q5A.

  (i) Describe the pattern of sulphur dioxide emissions shown on Reference Map Q5A.    **4**

**Reference Diagram Q5B: Factors affecting Environmental Quality of Air**

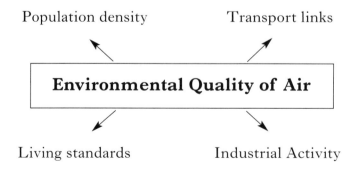

Population density      Transport links

**Environmental Quality of Air**

Living standards      Industrial Activity

  (ii) Give reasons for the pattern you have described in part (*a*)(i).

     You may refer to the factors shown in Diagram Q5B.    **4**

*Marks*

5. **(continued)**

**Reference Diagram Q5C: European Water Supply—Key Facts**

| 20% of all surface water is seriously threatened with pollution |
| Groundwater supplies 65% of all Europe's drinking water |

Area of irrigated land in Southern Europe has increased by 20% since 1985

(b) Study Reference Diagram Q5C.

(i) For any river you have studied **describe** the strategies used to maintain or improve its water quality. **4**

(ii) Comment on how effective these strategies have been. **3**

**(15)**

**[Turn over**

*Mar*

## Question 6: Development and Health

### Reference Map Q6A: World Energy Consumption

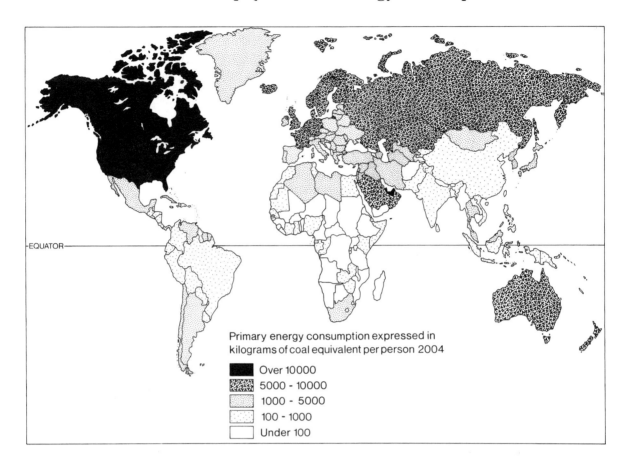

Primary energy consumption expressed in
kilograms of coal equivalent per person 2004

| | |
|---|---|
| ■ | Over 10000 |
| ▨ | 5000 - 10000 |
| ▤ | 1000 - 5000 |
| ▨ | 100 - 1000 |
| □ | Under 100 |

(*a*)  Study Reference Map Q6A.

Describe the pattern of energy consumption.                                **4**

### Reference Diagram Q6B: Human Factors affecting Level of Development

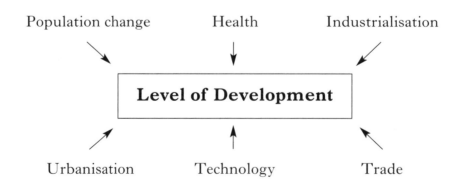

Population change        Health        Industrialisation

**Level of Development**

Urbanisation        Technology        Trade

(*b*)  Study Reference Diagram Q6B.

How do human factors such as those shown on the diagram affect the level of
development of a country?                                                    **6**

(*c*)  What are the main causes of **either** malaria **or** AIDS?            **5**

                                                                           **(15)**

*Marks*

**Question 7: Environmental Hazards**

**Reference Map Q7A:  Pakistan Earthquake, October 2005**

(*a*)  Study Reference Map Q7A.

For this, or any other earthquake you have studied, **explain** the main causes of the earthquake.

3

**[Turn over for Questions 7(*b*) and (*c*) on *Page eighteen***

*Mar*

7.    **(continued)**

**Reference Diagram Q7B:  Comparison of similar Richter Scale Earthquakes**

| **Pakistan Earthquake** |
| --- |
| October 2005 |
| Richter Scale   7·6 |
| Deaths          79 000 |
| Injured         75 038 |

| **San Francisco Earthquake** |
| --- |
| October 1989 |
| Richter Scale   7·1 |
| Deaths          63 |
| Injured         3757 |

(*b*)  Study Reference Diagram Q7B.

   **Explain** why earthquakes of similar strength have different effects on the landscape and population in the areas affected.                                                                              5

(*c*)  (i)  For a Tropical Storm you have studied, how effective were the warnings given in helping to reduce the impact of the storm?

   Give reasons for your answer.                                                                              4

   (ii)  What help was given to the people in the area immediately after the storm in part (*c*)(i)?                                                                              3

                                                                              **(15)**

*[END OF QUESTION PAPER]*

FOR OFFICIAL USE

| | | | | | |
|---|---|---|---|---|---|
| | | | | | |

# X208/203

NATIONAL
QUALIFICATIONS
2008

THURSDAY, 22 MAY
9.00 AM – 11.00 AM

GEOGRAPHY
INTERMEDIATE 2
Worksheet Q2(*b*)(i)

---

**Fill in these boxes and read what is printed below.**

Full name of centre

Town

Forename(s)

Surname

Date of birth
Day   Month   Year      Scottish candidate number      Number of seat

To be inserted inside the front cover of the candidate's answer book
and returned with it.

---

**WORKSHEET Q2(*b*)(i)**

## SCATTERGRAPH

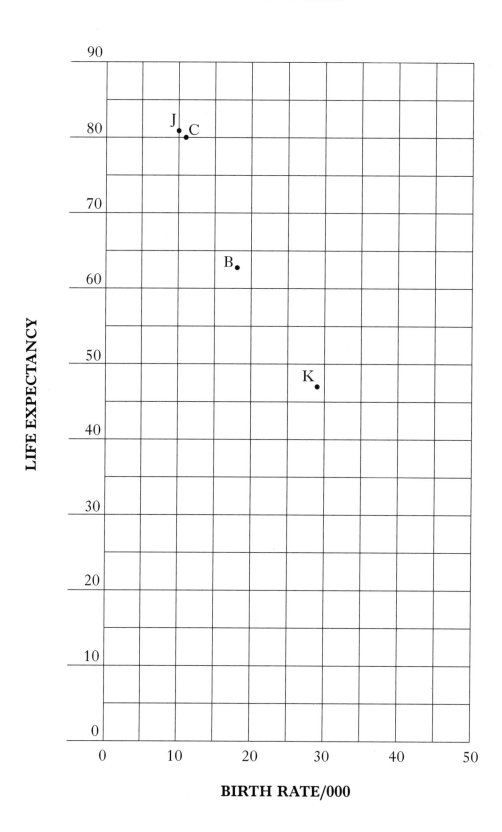

[*END OF WORKSHEET*]

# 2009

[BLANK PAGE]

# X208/201

NATIONAL
QUALIFICATIONS
2009

WEDNESDAY, 27 MAY
9.00 AM – 11.00 AM

# GEOGRAPHY
INTERMEDIATE 2

Candidates should answer **four** questions:

| | | |
|---|---|---|
| | Section A | Question 1 **and** Question 2 |
| **AND** | | |
| | Section B | any **two** questions from Questions 3 to 7 |

Candidates should read the questions carefully. Answers should be clearly expressed and relevant.

Credit will always be given for appropriate sketch-maps and diagrams.

Write legibly and neatly, and leave a space of about one cm between the lines.

All maps and diagrams in this paper have been printed in black only: no other colours have been used.

1:25 000 Scale
Explorer Series

OL2

392000m

467000m

66

431

Ford

Are
Shake

65

Shake
Hole

64

Great
ld Knott
Settlement
field Sys
s Lane
g House

63

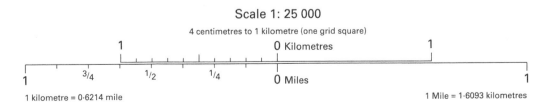

Scale 1: 25 000

4 centimetres to 1 kilometre (one grid square)

| 1 | | 0 Kilometres | | 1 |

1 kilometre = 0·6214 mile

1 Mile = 1·6093 kilometres

| 1 | 3/4 | 1/2 | 1/4 | 0 Miles | | 1 |

nlith Gill

h Moor

462000m

392000m

Extract produced by Ordnance Survey 2008.

*Mark*

## SECTION A

### IN THIS SECTION YOU <u>MUST</u> ANSWER QUESTION 1 <u>AND</u> QUESTION 2.

**Question 1:  Physical Environments**

### Reference Diagram Q1A

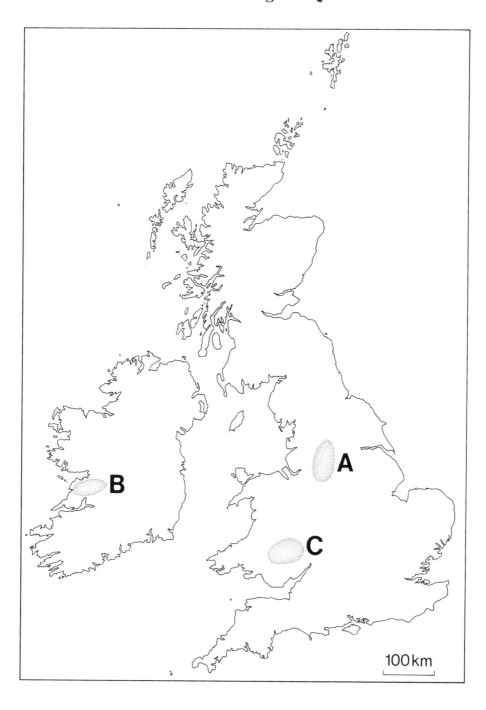

(*a*)  Look at Reference Diagram Q1A.

Name the **three** areas of upland limestone shown on the map.                    3

*Marks*

## 1. (continued)

(b) Study the Ordnance Survey Map Extract (No 1744/OL2).

(i) Match each of the following landscape features found on the map with the correct grid reference.

**Limestone pavement**      **Gorge**      **Shake Hole**      **Pot Holes**

Choose from:

Grid References      872662      914638      903647      873647      906654.      **4**

(ii) For **one** of the features mentioned above, **explain** how it was formed.

You may wish to use a diagram(s) in your answer.      **4**

### Reference Diagram Q1B

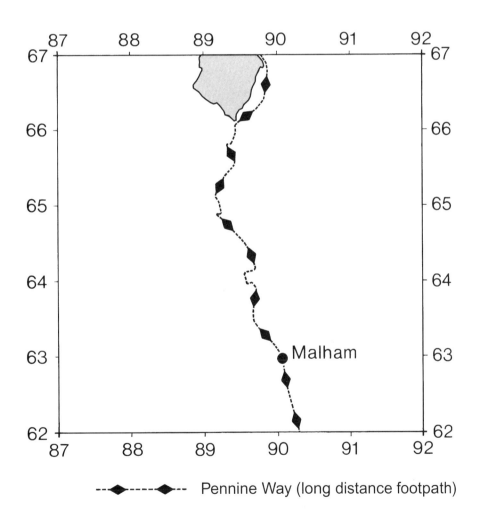

--◆-----◆-- Pennine Way (long distance footpath)

(iii) Study the Ordnance Survey Map Extract (No 1744/OL2) and Reference Diagram Q1B.

**Explain** why this is a suitable route for the Pennine Way.      **4**

*Mark*

1.    **(continued)**

**Reference Diagram Q1C**

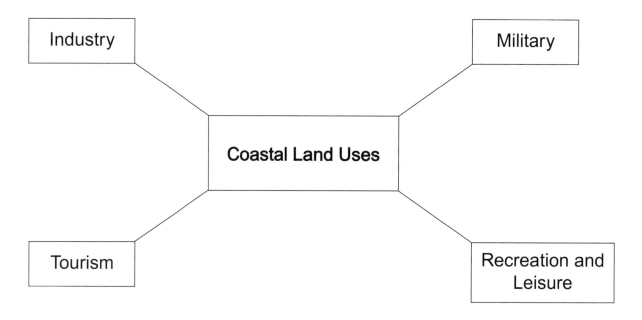

(c)    (i)    Select any **two** of the above land uses.

For a **coastal** area you have studied, describe the **economic benefits** and **environmental problems** for each land use selected.    6

(ii)    How do public **and** voluntary organisations try to reduce the problems you identified in part (i)?    4

**(25)**

*[END OF QUESTION 1]*

**NOW GO ON TO QUESTION 2**

*Marks*

## Question 2: Human Environments

### Reference Diagram Q2A: Population Pyramids for an Economically Less Developed Country (ELDC)

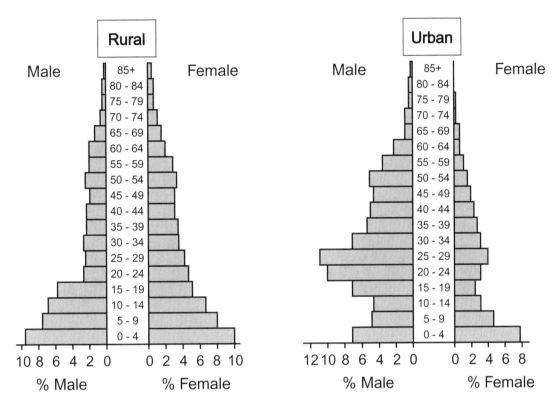

(a) Look at Reference Diagram Q2A.

(i) Describe the main **differences** in the population structures between the **rural** and **urban** areas, shown in Reference Diagram Q2A, in an ELDC.    **3**

(ii) Suggest reasons for the differences you described in (a)(i).    **4**

### Reference Diagram Q2B: Infant Mortality Statistics

| Country | Infant Mortality per 1000 live Births |
|---|---|
| USA | 6 |
| UK | 5 |
| India | 54 |
| Bangladesh | 60 |

(b) **Explain** why Economically More Developed Countries (EMDCs) have a low infant mortality rate.    **3**

**[Turn over**

*Mark*

2.  **(continued)**

### Reference Diagram Q2C

(c)  For any named Economically Less Developed city you have studied, describe measures taken to improve the quality of life in shanty towns.    **5**

### Reference Diagram Q2D:  Recent Changes in Agriculture in Economically Less Developed Countries (ELDCs)

| Increased use of Chemical fertilisers | Increased Mechanisation |
|---|---|

(d)  What benefits **and** problems have changes such as those shown in the diagram brought to ELDCs?    **5**

*Marks*

2. **(continued)**

**Reference Diagram Q2E: Nueva Condomina—Murcia in Spain**

The shopping centre includes a 15 screen multiplex and a 13 700 m² Hypermarket. There is parking for 6500 cars.

(e) What are the advantages **and** disadvantages of this or any other Edge of Town shopping development you have studied?

5

**(25)**

*[END OF SECTION A]*

**NOW TURN TO SECTION B AND ANSWER TWO QUESTIONS**

**[BLANK PAGE]**

## SECTION B

**Environmental Interactions**

**Answer any two questions from this section.**

Choose from

**[Turn over**

**SECTION B**

*Mark*

## Question 3: Rural Land Degradation

**Reference Diagram Q3A: Sokoto, Nigeria**

**Location**

**Reference Diagram Q3B: Sokoto, Nigeri.**

**Climate**

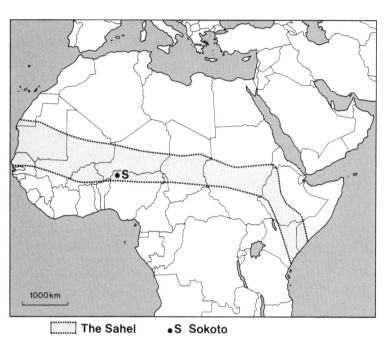

The Sahel    •S  Sokoto

1000km

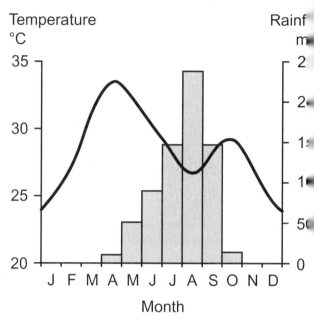

(*a*)   (i)   Study Reference Diagrams Q3A and Q3B above.

**Explain** why the climate of Sokoto might cause desertification in the surrounding area.

3

*Marks*

3.  **(a) (continued)**

### Reference Diagram Q3C: Desertification

(ii)  Study Reference Diagram Q3C.

Some countries are trying to reduce desertification.

(*a*)  Describe the methods used.

(*b*)  Do you think these methods are successful?

Explain your answer.    **4**

(*b*)  (i)  For a forested area you have studied, describe how farming can lead to land degradation.    **4**

(ii)  Describe what can be done to prevent deforestation.    **4**

    **(15)**

**[Turn over**

**Question 4:  River Basin Management**

**Reference Diagram Q4A:  Physical Characteristics of a River Basin**

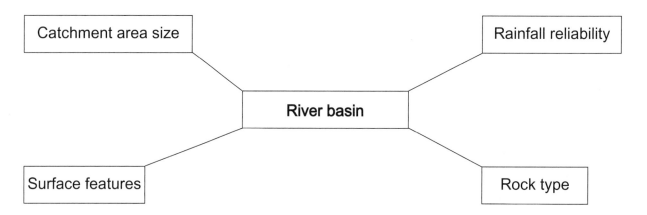

Catchment area size

Rainfall reliability

River basin

Surface features

Rock type

(*a*)  Study Reference Diagram Q4A.

Why are some river basins better suited to water management projects than others?    **4**

**Reference Diagram Q4B:  Nile River Basin**

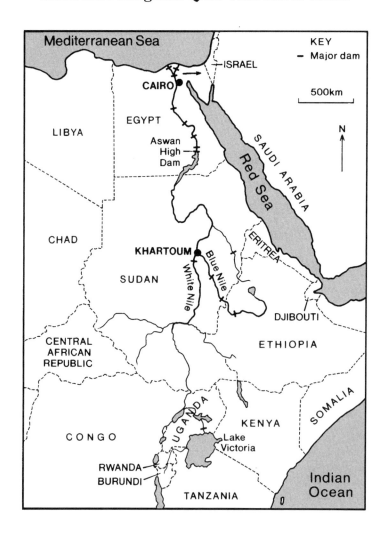

(*b*)  Study Reference Diagram Q4B.

For the Nile River basin, or any other river you have studied, what are the benefits of managing the river?    **4**

*Marks*

4.    (continued)

### Reference Diagram Q4C:  Murray–Darling River Basin

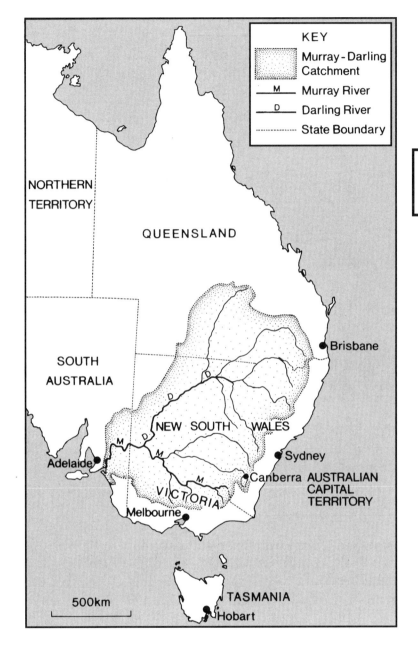

2,000,000 householders live in the Murray—Darling river basin area.

(*c*)   Study Reference Diagram Q4C.

   (i)   What factors, other than household use, can increase the demand for water? Give reasons for your answer.    **4**

   (ii)   Water control projects can cause political problems.  Describe some of these problems.    **3**

**(15)**

**[Turn over**

*Mark*

**Question 5: European Environmental Inequalities**

**Reference Map Q5A: Selected European Coastal Areas and Rivers under Environmental Pressure**

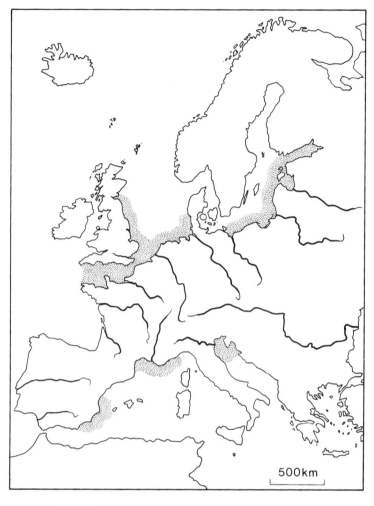

**Key**        Coastal Area under Environmental Pressure

Polluted Rivers

(a)  Study Reference Map Q5A.

Coastal areas are under increasing environmental pressure.

Referring to economic **and** social factors, **explain** why such areas are under threat.                    **5**

(b)  For any **two** rivers you have studied, **explain** differences in their environmental quality.                    **3**

(c)  (i)  What methods have been used to improve environmental quality in either a coastal or mountain area you have studied?                    **4**

(ii)  Have these methods been successful?

Give reasons for your answer.                    **3**

**(15)**

*Marks*

## Question 6: Development and Health

### Reference Diagram Q6A: Levels of Wealth and Life Expectancy

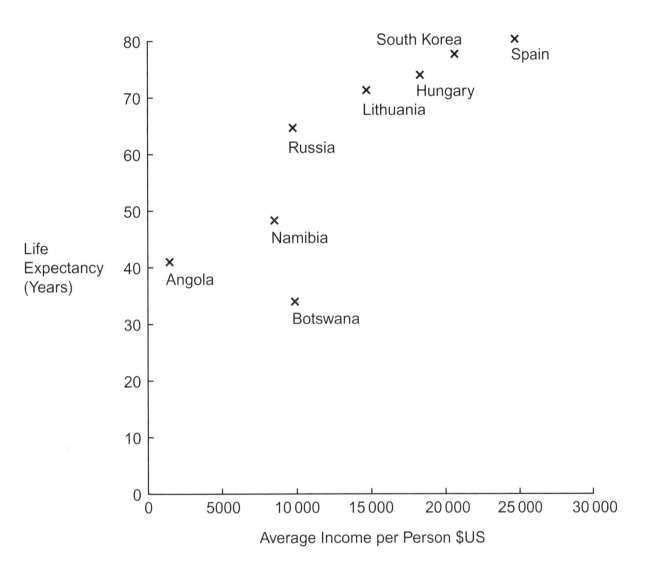

(*a*) Study Reference Diagram Q6A.

   (i) Describe **in detail** the relationship between average income and life expectancy.       **3**

   (ii) Why are combined indicators such as the Human Development Index (HDI) more reliable methods of measuring a country's overall level of development?       **4**

(*b*)  (i) For heart disease **or** malaria, what are the consequences of the disease for the population in an affected area?       **4**

   (ii) For the disease chosen in (*b*)(i), how successful are the methods used to control it?

     Explain your answer.       **4**

                 **(15)**

**[Turn over**

*Mark*

## Question 7:  Environmental Hazards

### Reference Diagram Q7A:  Pacific Ring of Fire

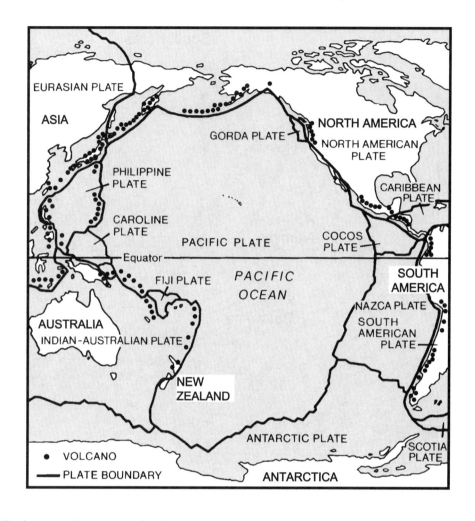

(a)  Study Reference Diagram Q7A.

**Explain** the distribution of tectonic activity in the area shown.     **3**

(b)  Referring to an earthquake **or** volcanic eruption you have studied:

(i)   describe methods of predicting the hazard;     **3**

(ii)  **explain** the importance of both short term **and** long term aid in reducing the effects of the hazard.     **4**

(c)  For a named tropical storm you have studied, describe **in detail** its impact on the landscape **and** population.     **5**

**(15)**

*[END OF QUESTION PAPER]*

[BLANK PAGE]

# X208/201

NATIONAL
QUALIFICATIONS
2010

MONDAY, 31 MAY
9.00 AM – 11.00 AM

GEOGRAPHY
INTERMEDIATE 2

Candidates should answer **four** questions:

Section A    Question 1
**and**
Question 2

**AND**

Section B    any **two** questions from
Questions 3 to 7

Candidates should read the questions carefully. Answers should be clearly expressed and relevant.

Credit will always be given for appropriate sketch-maps and diagrams.

Write legibly and neatly, and leave a space of about one cm between the lines.

All maps and diagrams in this paper have been printed in black only: no other colours have been used.

1:50 000 Scale
Landranger Series

Four colours should app
Four colours should app

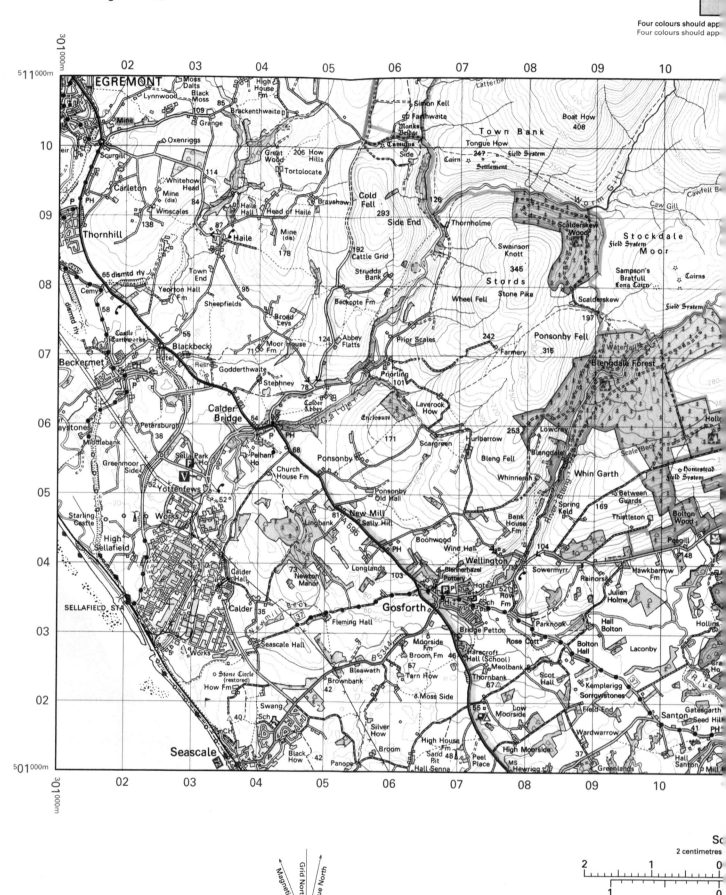

Grid North
True North
Magnetic North

Diagrammatic only

Sc
2 centimetres

1 kilometre = 0·6214 mile

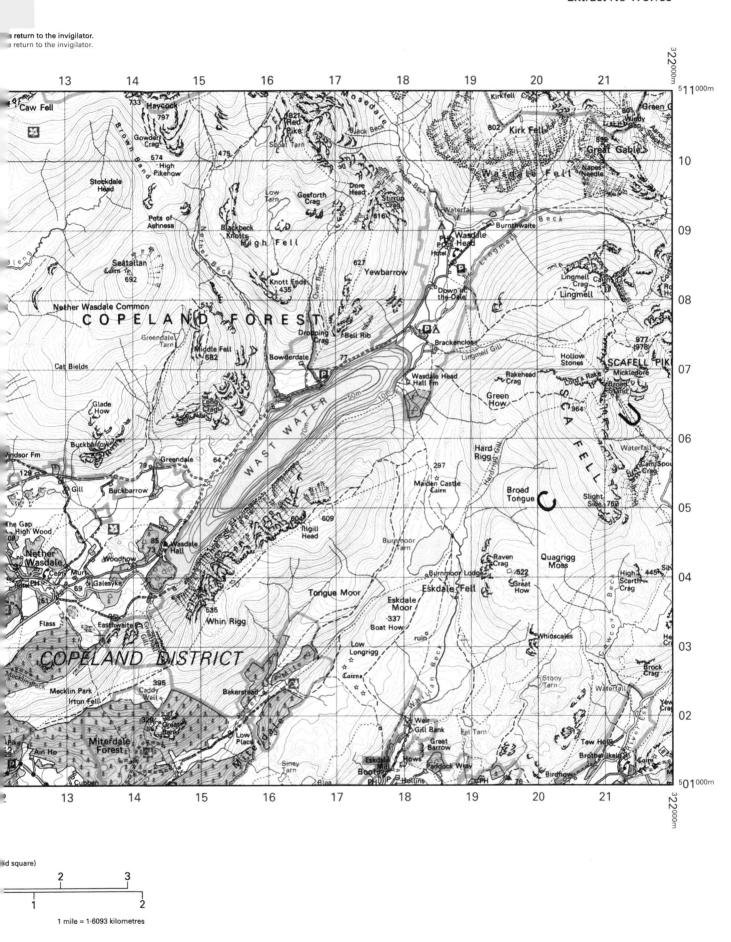

1 mile = 1·6093 kilometres

*Mark*

## SECTION A

## IN THIS SECTION YOU <u>MUST</u> ANSWER QUESTION 1 <u>AND</u> QUESTION 2.

**Question 1: Physical Environments**

### Map Q1A: Selected Landscapes in Scotland

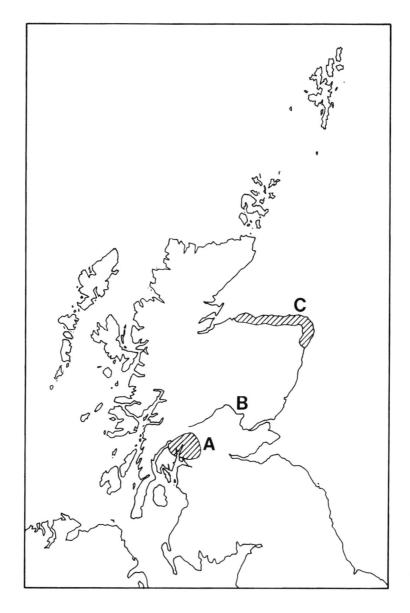

(a)   Look at Map Q1A.

Name:

   (i)   glaciated upland area A;

  (ii)   river B;

  (iii)   coastal area C.

3

*Marks*

1. **(continued)**

(b) Study the Ordnance Survey Map Extract (No 1787/89).

   (i) Match these glaciated features with the correct grid reference.

   **Truncated spur      Arête      Corrie      Hanging Valley**

   Choose from:

   Grid References      159103      139084      135057      183097      206068.      **4**

   (ii) Wast Water (1505) is an example of a ribbon lake.

   How were ribbon lakes formed?

   You may wish to use a diagram(s) in your answer.      **4**

(c) Describe the physical features of the River Calder **and** its valley from Monks Bridge (064103) to where it meets the A595 at Calder Bridge (043060).      **4**

### Diagram Q1B: Land Uses in Coastal and Upland Areas

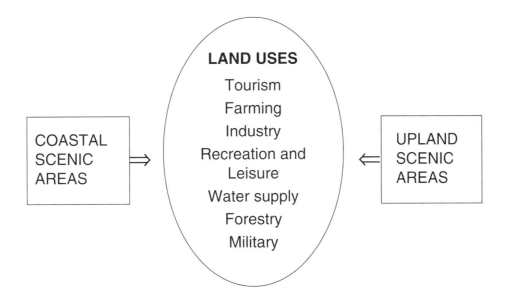

(d) Study Diagram Q1B.

   For an upland **or** coastal area you have studied, explain, **in detail**, ways in which some of the land uses shown may be in conflict with each other.      **6**

(e) How do various organisations try to protect areas of outstanding scenery in the UK?      **4**

      **(25)**

*[END OF QUESTION 1]*

**NOW GO ON TO QUESTION 2**

*Mark*

**Question 2:  Human Environments**

### Diagram Q2A:  Projected World Population and Population Growth Rate 1950–2050

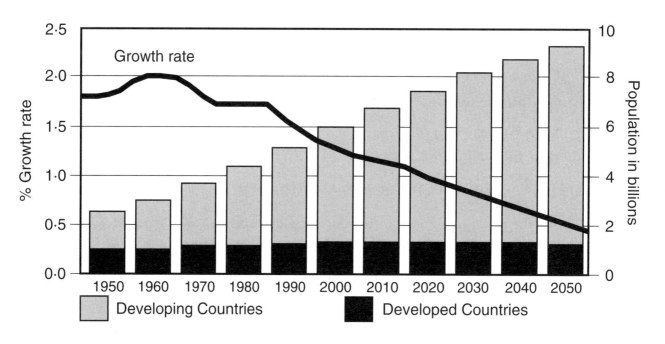

(*a*)    Study Diagram Q2A.

   (i)    Describe changes in the projected World Population Growth Rate from 1950 to 2050.    **3**

   (ii)    What is the main difference in population growth between developing and developed countries?

   Give reasons for this difference.    **6**

*Marks*

2.    **(continued)**

**Diagram Q2B:  Population Pyramids for Kenya and Italy 2008**

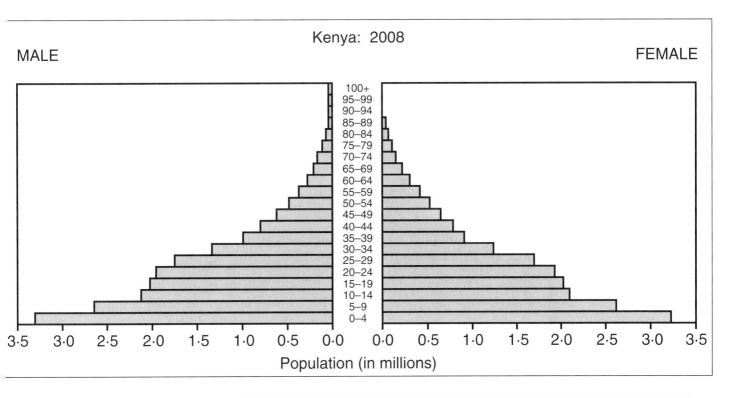

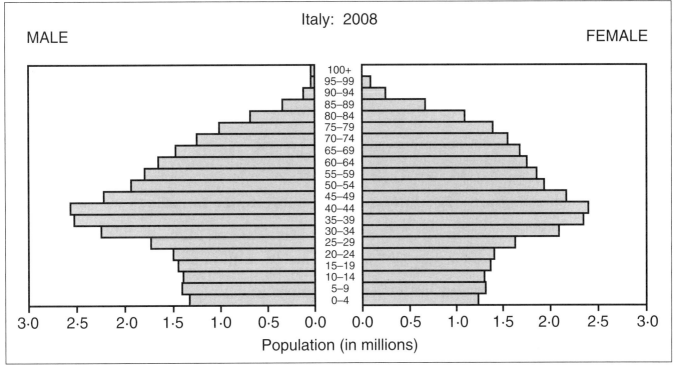

(*b*)    Study Diagram Q2B.

For Kenya **or** Italy describe the population structure.                                4

**[Turn over**

*Mark*

**2.    (continued)**

### Diagram Q2C:  Urban Sprawl

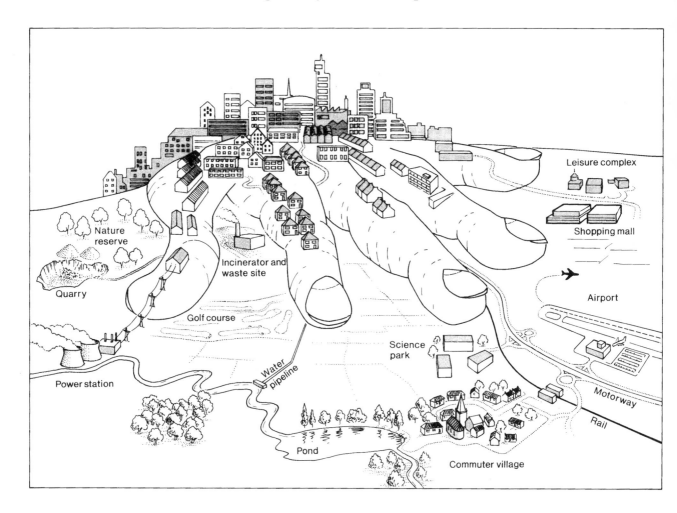

(*c*)    Study Diagram Q2C.

What effects does urban sprawl have on rural areas?                    **4**

### Diagram Q2D:  Effects of Green Revolution in India

> **Indian Rice production 2007/08 at record 94 million tons.**
>
> **Rice Yield at record 3·21 tons per hectare.**

(*d*)    **Explain** how countries such as India have been able to rapidly increase crop production.                    **4**

*Marks*

2.    **(continued)**

### Diagram Q2E:  Malaysia

**Airports in Malaysia**

**Location of Malaysia**

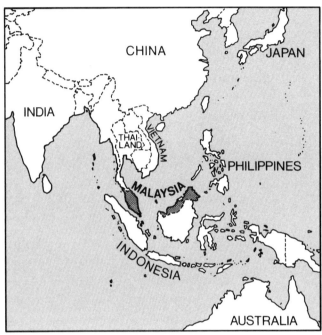

---

"Malaysia now has one of south-east Asia's most successful economies."

BBC Spokesperson, March 2010

---

(e)    Study Diagram Q2E.

**Explain** why many international companies are now locating their factories in developing countries such as Malaysia.

**4**

**Total    (25)**

*[END OF SECTION A]*

**NOW TURN TO SECTION B AND ANSWER TWO QUESTIONS**

# SECTION B

**Environmental Interactions**

**Answer any two questions from this section.**

Choose from

*Marks*

**SECTION B**

**Question 3:  Rural Land Degradation**

**Map Q3A:  S E Asia—Changes in Forest Cover 1985–2005**

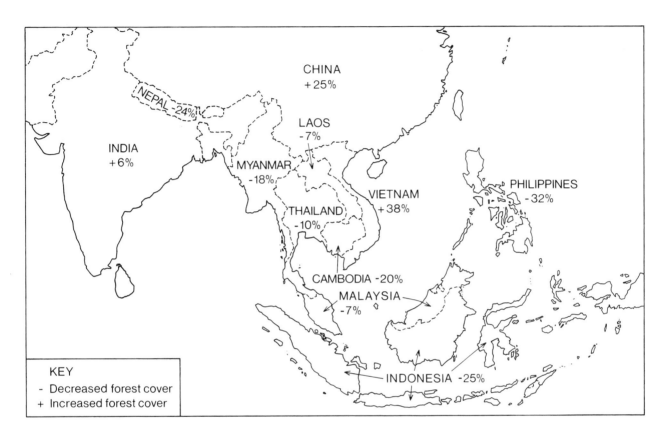

(*a*)    Study Map Q3A.

    (i)    Describe, **in detail**, changes in forest cover in South East Asia.          4

    (ii)    Referring to South East Asia, or any forest area you have studied, **explain** why forest cover has been removed.          4

(*b*)    **Explain** the main physical **and** human causes of desertification.          4

(*c*)    How can desertification be reduced?          3

                                      **Total    (15)**

**[Turn over**

*Mark*

**Question 4:  River Basin Management**

**Diagram Q4A:  Glen Canyon Dam USA**

(*a*)    For any river basin you have studied, describe in detail the physical factors which affect the amount of water which can be stored.      **4**

*Marks*

**4.** **(continued)**

**Diagram Q4B: Information on Dams in Amazon Region**

**Diagram Q4C: Local Protest against Dam Construction**

Brazil to spend $15·6 billion on dams in Amazon Region (Government source 2008)

(b) Study Diagrams Q4B and Q4C.

For this **or** any other River Basin project you have studied, **explain**:

 (i) why there was a need for the project;                                             4

 (ii) why some local people were opposed to the project.                              3

(c) Describe the economic and social benefits of this or any other project you have studied.                                                                                   4

                                                                                      **(15)**

**[Turn over**

*Marl*

**Question 5:  European Environmental Inequalities**

**Map Q5A:  Severely polluted European Rivers**

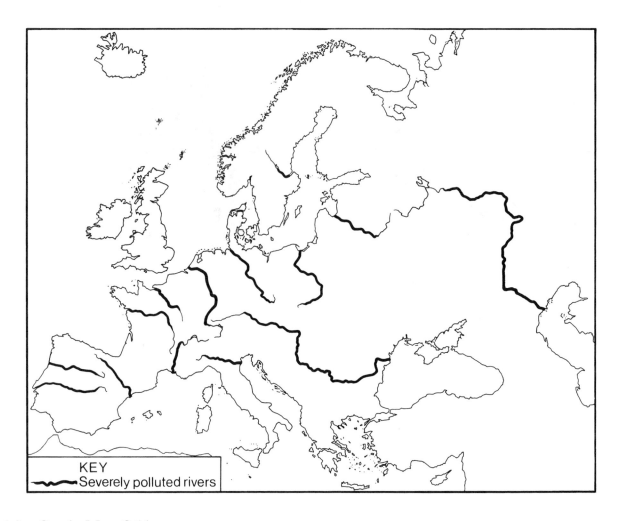

(*a*)    Study Map Q5A.

     (i)    Describe the distribution of severely polluted rivers in Europe.      **3**

     (ii)    Many rivers in Europe flow through farming and industrial areas.

         How do farming **and** industry cause river pollution?      **5**

*Marks*

5.   (continued)

### Diagram Q5B:  Air Pollution

(*b*)   Study Diagram Q5B.

    (i)   Describe different methods European countries have used to tackle the problem of air pollution.      **4**

    (ii)   To what extent have these methods been successful?      **3**

        **(15)**

**[Turn over**

*Marl*

**Question 6: Development and Health**

**Diagram Q6A: Physical Factors affecting Development**

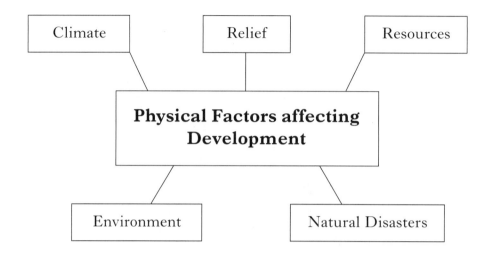

(a) Referring to the diagram above, describe how physical factors can affect the level of a country's development.    **4**

*Marks*

6.   (continued)

### Map Q6B:  People living with AIDS

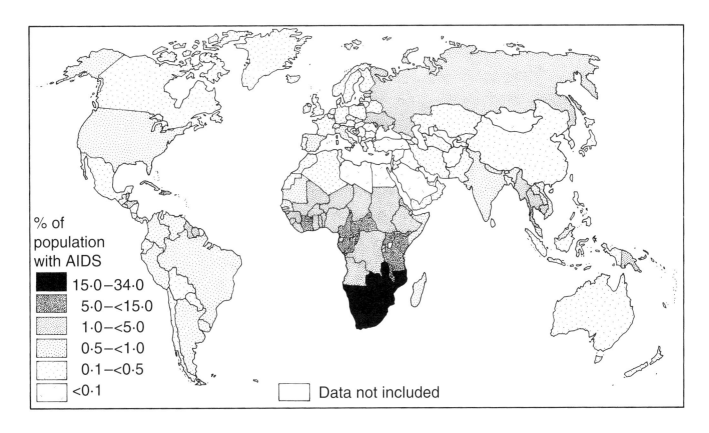

Study Map Q6B.

(b)   (i)   Describe, **in detail**, the distribution of people with AIDS throughout the
world.                                                                                                   4

(ii)   For AIDS **or** heart disease, describe attempts made to control the spread of
the disease.                                                                                          4

(iii)   Have these efforts been effective?

**Explain** your answer.                                                                         3

(15)

**[Turn over**

*Mark*

## Question 7: Environmental Hazards

### Map Q7A: Path of Tropical Storms starting in the Caribbean Sea

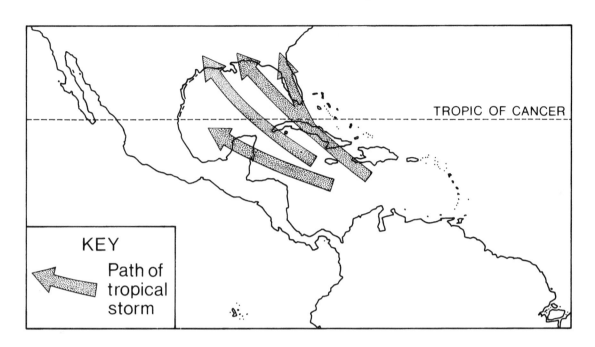

Study Map Q7A.

(*a*) Describe the movement of tropical storms shown on the map. **3**

### Diagram Q7B

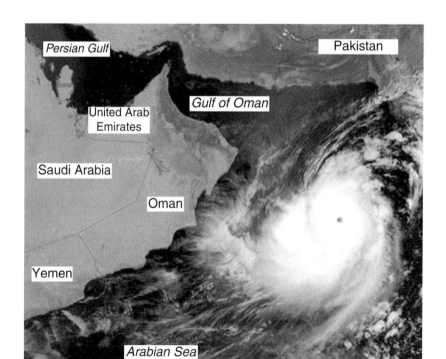

Look at Diagram Q7B

(*b*) **Explain** the main causes of tropical storms. **4**

*Marks*

**7. (continued)**

### Diagram Q7C: Earthquake Damage

Look at Diagram Q7C.

(*c*)  (i)  For an earthquake you have studied, describe the impact on the landscape **and** the local population.                                             **4**

(ii)  Describe ways in which the effects of an earthquake can be reduced.       **4**

**(15)**

*[END OF QUESTION PAPER]*

[BLANK PAGE]

[BLANK PAGE]

# X208/201

NATIONAL
QUALIFICATIONS
2011

TUESDAY, 24 MAY
9.00 AM – 11.00 AM

# GEOGRAPHY
# INTERMEDIATE 2

Candidates should answer **four** questions:    Section A    Question 1
**and**
Question 2

**AND**

Section B    any **two** questions from
Questions 3 to 7

Candidates should read the questions carefully.    Answers should be clearly expressed and relevant.

Credit will always be given for appropriate sketch-maps and diagrams.

Write legibly and neatly, and leave a space of about one cm between the lines.

All maps and diagrams in this paper have been printed in black only:  no other colours have been used.

Extract No 1881/158
1:50 000 Scale
Landranger Series

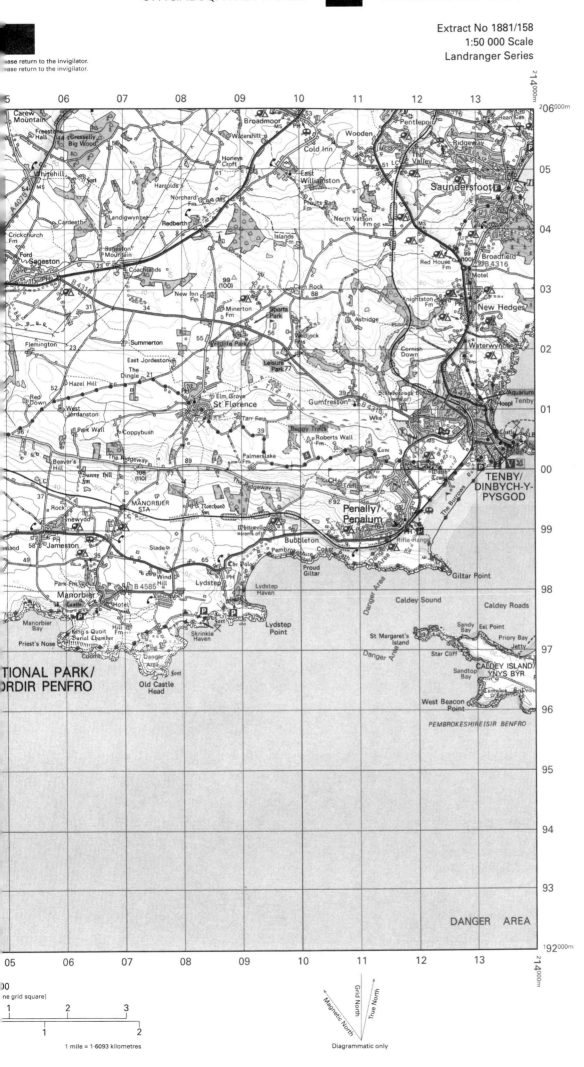

*Mar*

## SECTION A

### IN THIS SECTION YOU <u>MUST</u> ANSWER QUESTION 1 <u>AND</u> QUESTION 2.

**Question 1: Physical Environments**

**Map Q1A: Scenic Areas in the British Isles**

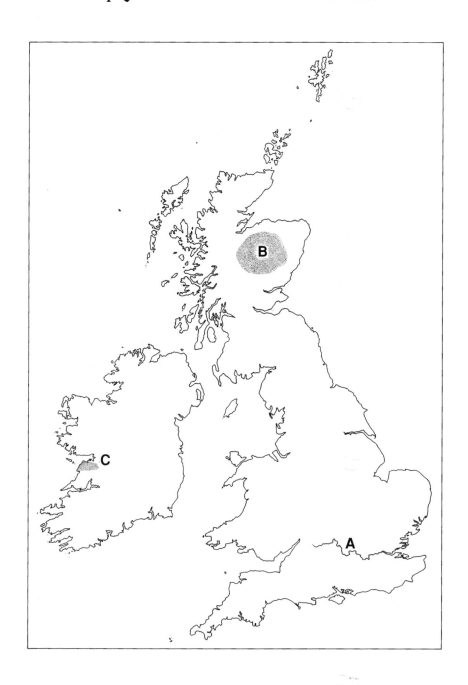

(a)   Look at Map Q1A.

   Name:

   (i)   the river at A;

   (ii)   area of upland glaciation B;

   (iii)   area of limestone C.

3

*Marks*

1.  **(continued)**

**Diagram Q1B: Barafundle Bay (Grid Reference 9995)**

(b)   Study the Ordnance Survey Map Extract (No 1881/158) and Diagram Q1B.

**Explain** the formation of headlands **and** bays.

You may wish to use diagrams.                                                4

**[Turn over**

*Mark*

1. **(continued)**

**Diagram Q1C: Pembroke**

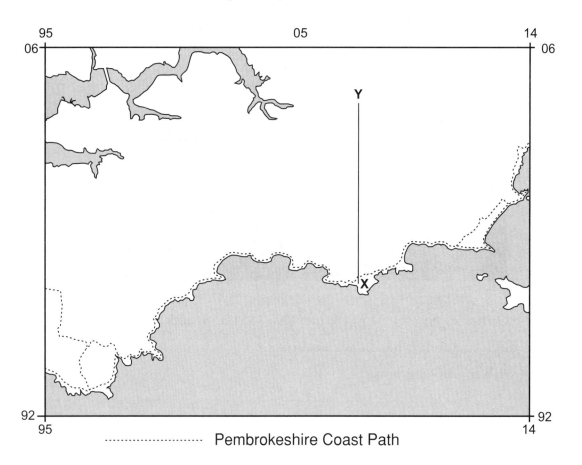

-------------------- Pembrokeshire Coast Path

**Diagram Q1D: Cross Section from GR 073970 to GR 073040**

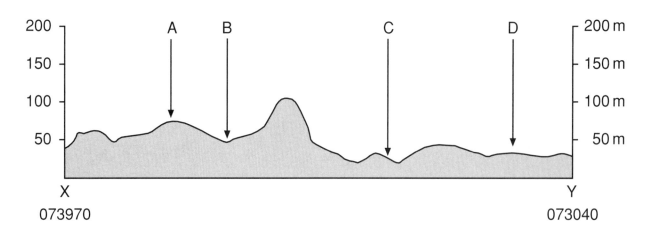

(c)  (i)  Look at the Ordnance Survey Map and Diagrams Q1C and Q1D.

Match the letters (A, B, C and D) on the cross section above with the correct feature below.

**Cycle Path    Railway    A4139    Forestry    National Trail**    4

(ii)  The Pembrokeshire coast path attracts a lot of walkers to the area.

Using map evidence, **explain** why.    4

*Marks*

**1.  (continued)**

**Diagram Q1E:  Selected Land Uses in Upland Areas**

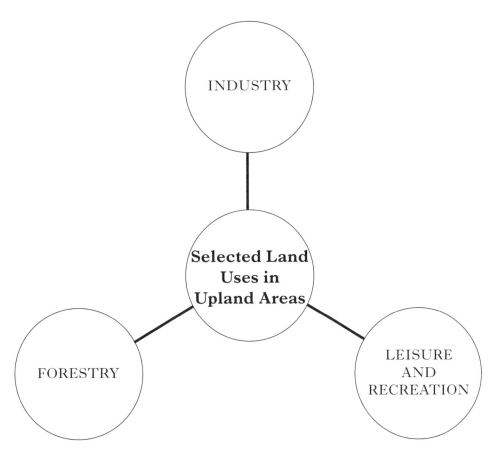

(*d*)  Study Diagram Q1E above.

For an upland area you have studied:

(i)  Choose **one** of the land uses shown in the diagram.  **Explain** the economic **and** environmental impact of the land use.    6

(ii)  What methods are used to reduce the environmental impact of your chosen land use?    4

**(25)**

*[END OF QUESTION 1]*

**NOW GO ON TO QUESTION 2**

**[Turn over**

*Mar*

**Question 2: Human Environments**

**Map Q2A: World Population Density**

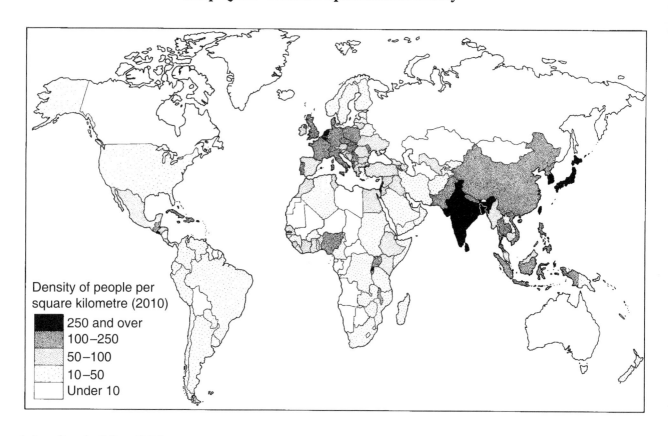

(*a*)    Study Map Q2A.

Referring to both **human** and **physical** factors, **explain** why some areas of the world are more densely populated than others.    **5**

*Marks*

2.    **(continued)**

**Diagram Q2B:  Population Pyramids, Scotland**

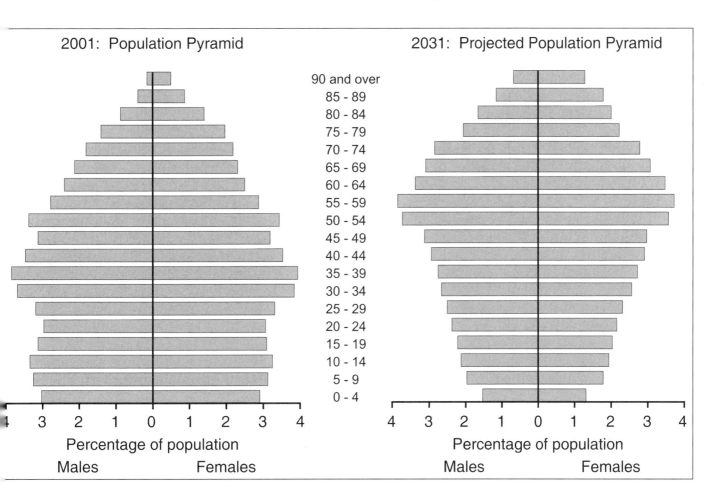

(*b*)    Study Diagram Q2B.

For Scotland, or any other country you have studied, describe problems which may
be caused by the population changes shown above.                                    5

**[Turn over**

*Mar*

2.    **(continued)**

### Diagram Q2C:  City Centre Traffic Congestion

(c)    Study Diagram Q2C.

For a city in a developed country you have studied:

(i)    what methods have been used to encourage people to use public transport;

(ii)    how successful have these methods been?    **6**

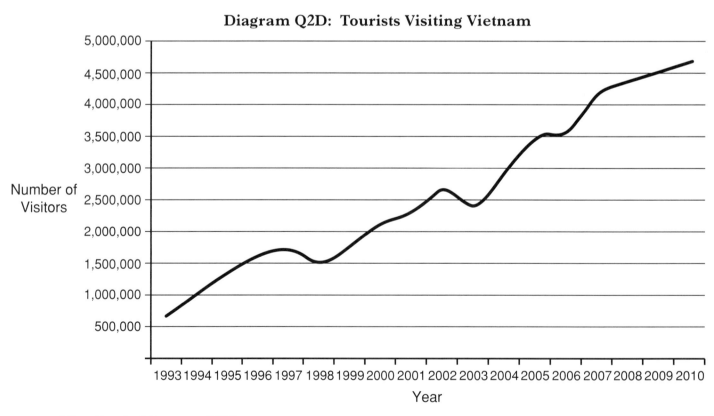

### Diagram Q2D:  Tourists Visiting Vietnam

(d)    Study Diagram Q2D.

Describe the benefits **and** problems caused by increased tourism in developing countries.    **5**

*Marks*

2.   **(continued)**

**Diagram Q2E: Old Industrial Landscape 1970**

**Diagram Q2F: New Industrial Landscape 2010**

(e)   Study Diagrams Q2E and Q2F.

Industrial landscapes in many areas have changed since 1970.

In what ways have these changes improved the environment?   **4**

**(25)**

*[END OF SECTION A]*

**NOW TURN TO SECTION B AND ANSWER TWO QUESTIONS**

## SECTION B

### Environmental Interactions

**Answer any two questions from this section.**

Choose from

*Marks*

## SECTION B

### Question 3: Rural Land Degradation

#### Diagram Q3A: Farming in the Sahel, Africa

(*a*)    Study Diagram Q3A.

**Explain** how traditional farming methods may lead to land degradation.    **6**

#### Diagram Q3B: Effects of Deforestation

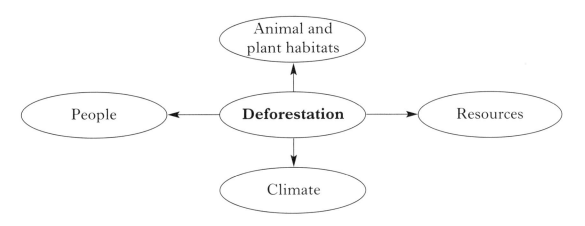

(*b*)    Study Diagram Q3B.

For an area you have studied:

(i)    describe the possible effects of deforestation;    **5**

(ii)    describe methods used to reduce deforestation.    **4**

**(15)**

**[Turn over**

*Mark*

**Question 4:  River Basin Management**

**Diagram Q4A:  The Hydrological Cycle**

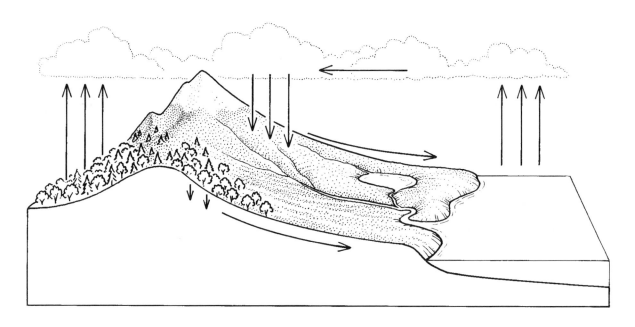

(a)    Study Diagram Q4A.

Describe, **in detail**, the processes taking place in the hydrological cycle.    **5**

**Diagram Q4B:  River Basin Features**

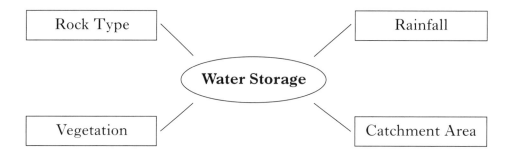

Study Diagram Q4B.

(b)    **Explain** how the features shown above can affect the amount of water which can be stored in a river basin.    **5**

(c)    For a water control project you have studied, **explain** the environmental problems which have resulted from the scheme.    **5**

**(15)**

**[Turn over for Question 5 on *Page fourteen***

*Marks*

### Question 5:  European Environmental Inequalities

**Map Q5A:  Levels of Air Pollution in Italy**

**Map Q5B:  Major Cities and Population Density in Italy**

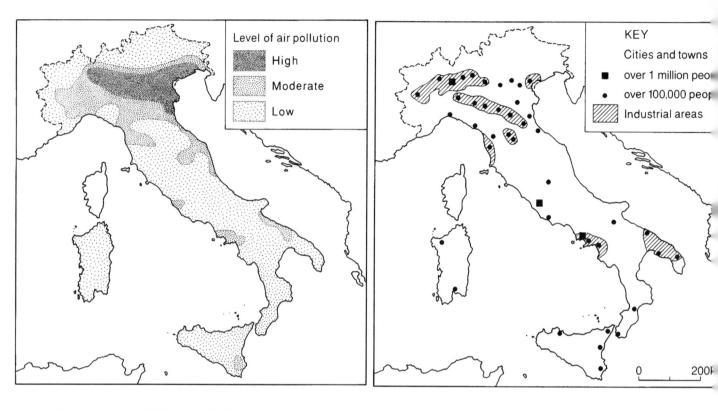

Study Maps Q5A and Q5B.

(*a*)   **Explain** the pattern of air pollution in Italy.                                    **4**

*Marks*

5.   **(continued)**

**Diagram Q5C: Factors Affecting Environmental Quality of Sea and Coastal Areas**

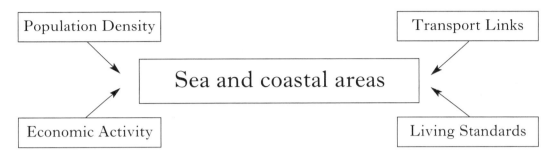

(b)   For a sea and coastal area you have studied, **explain** the different factors which can affect environmental quality.    **5**

**Diagram Q5D: European Rivers**

(c)   For any river you have studied:

   (i)   describe methods of improving or maintaining environmental quality;

   (ii)   how effective have these methods been?    **6**

**(15)**

**[Turn over**

*Mark.*

**Question 6: Development and Health**

### Map Q6: Human Development Index

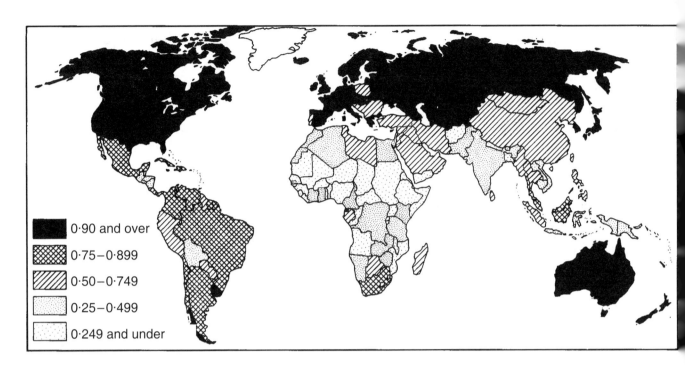

0·90 and over

0·75–0·899

0·50–0·749

0·25–0·499

0·249 and under

(*a*)    Study Map Q6.

Referring to both human **and** physical factors, **explain** why some countries are more developed than others.    **6**

(*b*)    Describe the main causes of either AIDS **or** heart disease.    **4**

(*c*)    For malaria **or** AIDS, what are the consequences of the disease for the population in an affected area?    **5**

**(15)**

*Marks*

## Question 7: Environmental Hazards

### Map Q7: Distribution of Volcanoes

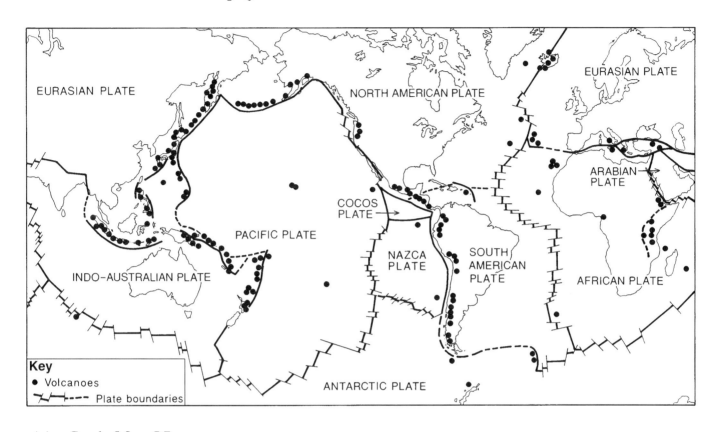

(a)   Study Map Q7.

   **Explain** the main causes of volcanic activity.    5

(b)   Describe methods used to predict volcanic eruptions and earthquakes.    4

(c)   For a tropical storm you have studied, **explain** the need for both long-term **and** short-term aid.    6

   **(15)**

*[END OF QUESTION PAPER]*

# Acknowledgements

Permission has been sought from all relevant copyright holders and Bright Red Publishing is grateful for the use of the following:

A map and population pyramid for Bangladesh taken from 'The New Wider World' by David Waugh. Reproduced with permission of David Waugh (2008 pages 5 & 6);

Two photographs of Centro Comercial Nueva Condomina. Reproduced with permission (2009 page 7);

Ordnance Survey © Crown Copyright. All rights reserved. Licence number 100049324.

**INTERMEDIATE 2 | ANSWER SECTION**

# SQA INTERMEDIATE 2
# GEOGRAPHY 2007–2011

## INTERMEDIATE 2 GEOGRAPHY 2007

## SECTION A
## PHYSICAL ENVIRONMENTS

1. (a) *For full marks both river features and valley must be mentioned.*
   Wide river (1), flowing through U-shape valley (1) in a North/North Easterly direction (1), flat floor and steep sides at first (1), meanders slightly (1), tributary joins at 624 662 (1), river meanders more as it flows North (1), island in river at 606 691 (1). Artificially straightened in 6166. Valley sides become lower and more gentle to the North (1).
   *Or any relevant point.* 4 marks

   (b) 662 622 = Corrie with tarn, (accept tarn only)
   645 610 = U-shaped valley
   673 653 = Pyramidal peak
   660 605 = Ribbon Lake
   Mark 4 = 3, 3 or 2 = 2, 1 = 1
   4 marks

   (c) Corrie
   *Full marks awarded to diagrams that clearly illustrate/explain formation.*
   Snow fills hollow, is compressed and turns to ice (1). Ice moves down hill under gravity (1), abrasion of corrie floor (1), plucking at backwall (1), deepens the hollow by erosion (1), lip left as ice loses power (1), freeze thaw at back helps steepen backwall (1).
   *Or any other relevant point.* 4 marks

   (d) *Answer will depend on land uses chosen. Maximum of 3 for 1 land use.*
   eg Quarrying spoils the environment (1) and does not fit in with promoting enjoyment of the area (1). Using up the rock does not promote long term use of a natural resource (1). Commercial Forestry is not a natural heritage (1), trees planted in straight lines do not help people enjoy area (1), when felled will spoil the natural environment (1).
   *Accept any relevant points.* 5 marks

   (e) (i) *Explanation is required for both benefits and problems for full marks.*
   Mark 3:2 or 2:3
   Benefits – employment eg hotels, B & Bs, lifeguards (1), money into area (1), social opportunities (1), facilities for locals eg leisure centres (1), beaches cleaned (1).
   Problems – increased traffic congestion (1), water and air pollution (1), second home ownership increases (1), litter on beach (1), sewage from caravan parks (1).
   *Or any other relevant points.*
   *Candidates must refer to both for full marks. Detailed description required.* 5 marks
   (ii) Local authorities fine for litter or dumping (1), restrict access (1), replant marram grass to conserve area (1), comply with EU Blue Flag Scheme (1), Voluntary litter picks (1), National Trust Conservation areas put in place (1), public education (1).
   *Or any other valid point.*
   *Both must be mentioned for full marks.* 4 marks
   **Total = 25 marks**

## HUMAN ENVIRONMENTS

2. (a) (i) Rural population has decreased from 72% to 52% (1). Urban has increased from 28% to 48% (1). Cities of 1 million+ have gone up from 9% to 21% (1).
   *If no data quoted, maximum 1 mark* 3 marks
   (ii) Increase in rural – urban migration (1) due to pull factors eg jobs (1) more money available (1) entertainment (1) etc.
   Push factors such as poverty in the countryside (1), drought and famine (1), poor housing/lack of medicine/education (1) etc.
   *Maximum 1 mark for simple list of push/pull factors.* 4 marks

   (b) Decreasing birth rate – shortage of trained workers (1), increased tax burden on working population (1), school closures (1).
   Increased life expectancy – large number of older dependants (1), increased health care costs (1), pressure on pension provision (1).
   *Or any other valid point.* 5 marks

   (c) *If no case study mentioned, mark out of four*
   Pedestrianisation to relieve traffic congestion (1), provide a safer environment (1) and to reduce pollution (1). Small independent shops replaced with larger chain stores (1) due to high costs in city centres (1). Covered shopping malls built to protect customers from weather (1).
   Accept negative points eg shop closure due to competition from out of town developments (1) etc.
   *Or any other valid point.*
   *Maximum 1 mark for a list of descriptive points only.*

   (d) Maximum of 1 mark for a list of descriptive points eg Set-aside land – overproduction and surpluses created (1) due to subsidies and incentives to farmers (1) and changes in customer demand (1). Land set-aside to reduce production levels (1).
   Animal Health Inspection – increase in bovine CJD (1) and outbreaks of foot and mouth disease (1). Prevention of disease spreading from imported animals (1). Maintain standards of quality in food supplies (1). 4 marks

   (e) *If no map evidence, mark out of three.*
   Mark 2:2, 1:3 or 3:1
   Flat land for building (1) and room for expansion (1). Near road and rail links for transport of materials and products (1). Close to urban area for labour supply and customers (1).
   *Accept negative points eg surrounded by road/rail/river therefore limited space for expansion (1).*
   Maximum of 1 mark for grid reference 4 marks
   **Total = 25 marks**

## SECTION B
## RURAL LAND DEGRADATION

3. (a) (i) Increasing population puts pressure on land (1), forest cleared for farmland (1) and housing (1). Use of trees for firewood (1) and charcoal for industry (1). Exploitation of minerals (1) such as bauxite or iron ore (1). Reference to HEP schemes for electricity (1).
   *Or any other valid point.* 5 marks

(ii) Create forest reserves (1), award National Park status to forest areas (1) avoid clear felling (1) select timber species for extraction (1), replant with fast growing trees (1). Publicity campaigns/ demonstrations by voluntary groups (1).
*Or any other valid point.*                              4 marks
Mark 3:3, 2:4 or 4:2

(b) *For full marks candidates must mention the physical and the human environment.*
*Physical:* increased soil erosion due to wind (1), less rainfall due to a reduction in evapo-transpiration (1) as vegetation is lost (1). More frequent sand and dust storms (1).
*Human:* farms/crops destroyed by sand (1) more human pressure on remaining farmland and forest (1), famine and malnutrition (1) forced migration out of affected areas (1).
*Or any other valid point.*                             6 marks
**Total = 15 marks**

## RIVER BASIN MANAGEMENT

4. (a) Size – large river basins will have more water flowing through them (1) and due to size will be able to store more water (1). Shape – steep river basins will have a quicker run-off than flatter (1).
Surface features – urban areas within river basin will have quicker movement of water due to concrete and drainage pipes (1). Rural areas may have slower movement due to vegetation eg forests (1).
Rock type – impermeable rock reduces infiltration (1) but may allow for more storage (1). Permeable rock will allow water to move through (1).
Rainfall distribution – mountain areas within the river basin tend to have higher rainfall and more water flow (1)
                                                        6 marks

(b) *All processes for full marks. Simple list 1 mark only.*
A – Transpiration – plants give off moisture (1) which evaporates into the air (1).
B – Evaporation – sun heating water which turns to water vapour (1).
C – Precipitation – no more moisture can be absorbed, clouds saturated (1) rain falls (1).
Accept 'infiltration'.
*Or any other valid point.*                             4 marks

(c) *Explanation needed for full marks. People and environment must be included for full marks. At least two benefits included for full marks. 5 × 1 for each relevant point.*
Irrigation – farmers can use water to grow more crops (1) and make more money (1).
Flood Control – towns have control over previous natural hazard (1), prevents loss of life (1) and damage to environment (1).
HEP – provides electricity for industrial development (1), brings new jobs (1), enhances environment with recreational facilities (1).
Tourism – increased numbers of people visiting area (1), increase in income for local business (1), wildlife attracted (1).
                                                        5 marks
**Total = 15 marks**

## EUROPEAN ENVIRONMENTAL INEQUALITIES

5. (a) (i) *Only 1 example needed for a mark.*
High levels are found in Southern Poland and bordering Germany, Slovakia and the Czech Republic. (1).
Medium levels are found in Poland, Germany, Sweden, Finland and north-east England. (1).
Low levels are found mainly in Germany and eastern Poland. (1).

Other parts of Europe do not appear to be affected by acid rain (1).                                     3 marks

(ii) *Both economic and climate required for full marks.*
Lot of industrial activity in west-central Europe eg NE France, Belgium, Germany and the UK. (1). Large centres of population in these same areas (1). Increased pollutants from traffic (1).
Prevailing south-westerly winds (1); moisture picked up in the Atlantic Ocean (1).                       4 marks
Mark 1:3, 2:2 or 3:1

(b) Less developed coastal areas eg Camargue: higher quality areas may be protected areas (1); may not be as suitable for development (1); may be in more isolated location (1).
More developed coastal areas eg Magaluf: lower quality areas due to too much development (1); developments may include tourism or industry (1); resultant pollution problems (1); visual pollution (1).
Less developed mountain areas eg Cairngorms: little development (1); explanation might include factors such as climate, location etc.
More developed mountain areas eg Zermatt: highly developed ski resort (1); dependable snow cover (1).
Maximum of 2 marks for description.                     4 marks

(c) Organisations such as the International Commission for the Protection of the Rhine established (1), by bordering countries such as France, Germany, Netherlands and Switzerland (1). Monitoring of fish stocks and water quality (1). Environmental pressure groups protest against dumping of toxic waste (1). This makes the public more aware (1). Improved sewage treatment (1). Limits set on dumping of dangerous chemicals (1). Companies which continue to pollute rivers are fined (1). Companies forced to build waste purification plants (1).
*Or any other valid points.*
*Maximum of 3 marks if no specific examples.*           4 marks
**Total = 15 marks**

## DEVELOPMENT AND HEALTH

6. (a) Indicators show only average figures (1) which hide wide variations within a country (1). The figure for one indicator may not be typical of the country's level of development (1) eg Saudi Arabia has a high GNP per capita, but the country is poorly developed in some areas (1). One indicator may hide wide variations between rich and poor (1) and also differences between areas within a country eg north-south divide (1) or between urban and rural areas (1). Certain indicators irrelevant to the real quality of life (1). Accept negative points concerning single indicators eg a country might score well in one but badly in another (1); combined indicators give a balance of both social and economic indicators (1); allows direct comparisons to be made between countries (1).
*Credit should also be given for specific examples.*    5 marks

(b) Mostly found in the developing world (1); Central America (1); Brazil and Columbia (1); Central Africa (1); south of the Sahara and north of South Africa (1); India and Pakistan (1); south-east Asia (1).                     3 marks

(c) (i) eg Malaria – use of insecticides (1) such as Malathion (1). Blood parasites treated with anti-malarial drugs (1) such as Chloroquine (1). Water released from dams to drown immature larvae (1). Genetic engineering of sterile male mosquitoes (1). Draining of breeding sites (1). Planting of eucalyptus trees to soak up moisture (1). Use of small fish to eat larvae (1). Mustard seeds to drag larvae below surface to drown them (1). Health education (1).

AIDS – Large-scale projects such as the Global AIDS initiative (1) and national treatment in South Africa (1). Increased funding to tackle the disease (1) from sources such as the World Bank (1). Drug therapy programmes (1). Attempts to develop AIDS vaccine (1). AIDS – awareness education (1). Tackling the disease through increased development of countries (1). Education campaigns advising of the risks of unprotected sex (1). Distribution of condoms (1). Encourage young people to abstain from sex until marriage (1).        4 marks

(ii) eg Malaria – Over 400 million people still suffer from the disease (1). Some insecticides eg Malathion, expensive to produce (1); unpopular as it leaves a nasty yellow colour (1) and has an unpleasant smell (1). Mosquitos have become resistant to some insecticides and anti-malarial drugs (1). Increased development in some areas has led to a return of malaria (1). Some insecticides harmful to the environment (1). Migration and growth of shanty towns has led to a return of the disease (1).

AIDS – still not enough funding (1); countries have other priorities (1); significant increases in funding in the last ten years (1). Drug therapy can produce serious side effects (1). Medication, so far, not very effective (1).        3 marks

**Total = 15 marks**

## ENVIRONMENTAL HAZARDS

**7.** (a) *Maximum 2 for descriptive points only.*
Formed over warm seas with temperatures over 27°C (1). Due to hotter temperatures between the tropics (1). Areas of extreme low pressure with rising air (1) and moist humid conditions (1). At least 5° North or South of the equator where the earth's rotation has more effect (1).        4 marks

(b) (i)   Reference should be made to casualties (1); inhabitants being made homeless (1); lack of food (1); destruction of buildings (1); damage by fire (1); disruption of telephone and electricity power lines (1); lack of water supplies (1); outbreak of disease (1). For full marks, reference should be made to a specific example, and to both people and the surrounding landscape.        4 marks

(ii)   Short-term aid: temporary shelter required for local people (1); emergency first aid will be required (1); more serious victims may need to be air lifted out of the area (1); supplies of blood, bandages etc… will be required (1); people may need to be provided with clothing (1); people will need immediate supplies of food and water (1).
Long-term aid: transport routes will need to be repaired (1); homes and other buildings will need to be rebuilt (1); power and communication lines will need to be re-instated (1).        4 marks

(iii)   Some attempt should be made to describe success or otherwise of the rescue operations. eg Huge loss of life after 2004 Tsunami (1). But tourist industry back up and running only a few months later (1). Difficulty in reaching victims of Pakistan earthquake due to remoteness and poor weather (1)
*Or any other valid point.*        3 marks

**Total = 15 marks**

## INTERMEDIATE 2 GEOGRAPHY 2008

## SECTION A
## PHYSICAL ENVIRONMENTS

**1.** (a) (i) *Full marks may be awarded for fully annotated diagrams. (max one mark for grid reference).*
8279 (cove/bay) harder rock protecting the coastline (1) is breached by hydraulic wave action (1) and corrasion/abrasion (1). Soft rock behind such as sandstone (1) is worn away more quickly than hard rock (1) creating a bay (1).
7780 (cliff/wave-cut platform) as waves strike the coast (1) land is eroded and undercut (1) by hydraulic action (1) and corrosion 1)/abrasion/ corrosion (1). Physical and chemical weathering affect the cliff face (1). Rock above becomes unstable and collapses (1) forming a cliff (1). Over time the cliff recedes (1) leaving a wave-cut platform at sea level (1).
*Also accept reference to White Nothe headland and headland formation.*        4 marks

(ii) *For full marks reference must be made to the river and its valley. (max one mark for grid reference).*
The river flows very slowly (1) in a south east to easterly direction (1). The river is meandering (1) and divides in several places (1) eg at 808892 (1). There is evidence of ox-bow lake formation (1) in square 8387 (1). The river flows in a flat flood plain (1) over 1km wide in places (1). The valley sides are gentle and low (1).        4 marks

(b) (i) A - Farming
B - Industry
C - Settlement
D - Military Training
4 correct = 3 marks. 2, 3 correct = 2 marks.
1 correct = 1 mark        3 marks

(ii) Noise from military training may disrupt livestock (1) or spoil the peace and quiet for tourists (1). Local and tourist traffic may be delayed by military vehicles (1). Walkers can be denied access to rights of way such as the South West Coast Path during training activities (1) eg in square 8580 (1). Local businesses, however, may be boosted by income from military personnel (1). Lower property prices (1).
*Or any other valid point.*        4 marks

(c) (i) *For full marks candidates must refer to both economic and environmental factors.*
Mark 3:3, 4:2 or 2:4
eg Hydro-electricity: farmland will be lost when valley is flooded (1). Construction equipment and vehicles will create noise pollution (1) and road congestion (1). The completed dam and pipelines cause visual pollution in the upland environment (1). Jobs will be provided during construction (1) increasing income in the local community (1). There will be a more reliable electricity supply in the area (1). Small businesses may be attracted to the area providing jobs (1).
*Or any other valid point.*        6 marks

(ii) National Park Authorities can refuse planning permission for developments which may cause conflict (1). Different recreational activities may be zoned (1) such as waterskiing and sailing (1). Park rangers are employed to prevent problems developing (1). NPA visitor centres educate the public about the Countryside

Code (1). One-way systems and pedestrianised areas are introduced (1) to reduce the effect of traffic congestion (1). Voluntary bodies such as the National Trust protects areas by buying land and buildings (1), maintaining walls and footpaths (1), and protecting important wildlife habitats (1).
*Or any other valid point.*                                    4 marks
**Total = 25 marks**

## HUMAN ENVIRONMENTS

2. (*a*) *Both physical and human factors should be mentioned for full marks.*
   Possible answers may include:
   Few people live where the climate is very cold (1). Few people live where there is very little rainfall (1). Few people live where there are very poor soils (1). Few people live where there are steep mountain ranges (1). Few people live where there are few or no resources (1). Few people live where transport systems are poor (1). Few people live where it is difficult to grow crops (1). Few people live where there are few employment opportunities (1).
   5 marks

   (*b*) (i) *4 countries plotted correctly - 2 marks*
   *2 / 3 countries plotted correctly - 1 mark*
   *0 or 1 country plotted correctly - 0 marks*          2 marks

   (ii) *The relationship must be stated for full marks. If not max 3.*
   The higher the birth rate the lower the life expectancy (1) (or vice versa).
   Possible reasons:
   Areas with high birth rate may include poor levels of health care (1). High birth rate may indicate high population growth, resulting in possible food shortage (1). High birth rate may be linked to occurrence of a number of diseases (1). High birth rate may indicate high levels of infant mortality (1). Poverty (1) example from graph (1).          4 marks

   (*c*) Possible answers may include:
   Improve the education of females (1).
   Introduce laws to limit the size of the family (1).
   Provide male sterilisation programmes (1). Increase the availability of family planning (1). Provide incentives for people to limit the size of their family (1).          4 marks

   (*d*) Possible answers may include:
   *Maximum of 4 if no named city.*
   The authorities sometimes provide the shell of a building with walls and roof (1); a water supply can be provided (1); local authorities sometimes provide toilet facilities (1); shanty town dwellers could develop small industries and businesses (1); schools may be provided in the shanty towns (1); people may be given the legal rights to the land (1); local residents may work together in self-help schemes (1).          5 marks

   (*e*) Regeneration of inner city areas (1); old slum housing pulled down (1); renovation of some tenements (1); new amenities/facilities such as toilets, central heating etc…(1); gentrification of run down areas (1); opening of new shopping centres (1); provision of desirable housing (1); planning restrictions in rural villages and coastal towns (1).
   5 marks
   **Total = 25 marks**

## SECTION B
## RURAL LAND DEGRADATION

3. (*a*) (i) Deforestation provides timber for export (1) or clears areas for food production (1) which can contribute to a country's income (1) and improve its balance of trade (1).
   *Or any other valid point.*

*People and environment must be mentioned for full marks.*
3 marks

(ii) Tribal people may lose their homes due to large scale deforestation (1) and may have to move to other areas (1). As tree cover is reduced wildlife habitats can be lost (1) and there may be increased soil erosion (1). Forest burning can create air pollution (1) and also contribute to global warming as $CO_2$ levels increase (1). Large scale clearance reduces transpiration (1) and the climate may become drier (1).
*Or any other valid point.*          4 marks

(*b*) (i) *Physical*
   - prolonged drought over a period of time (1)
   - failure of seasonal rains (1)
   - lack of cloud cover and higher temperatures (1)
   - effects of wind erosion (1).
   or
   *Human*
   - increasing population/expanding settlement (1)
   - increased demand for food (1)
   - over-cultivation/monoculture (1)
   - vegetation cut down for firewood (1)
   - over-grazing speeds up soil erosion   4 marks

(ii) eg in Sahel areas: methods could include:
   - stabilisation of dunes with fencing (1) and lines of drought resistant plants such as cactus (1)
   - contour ploughing to reduce gully erosion (1)
   - 'magic stones' along level lines to prevent surface runoff (1)
   - crop rotation and fallowing to retain soil fertility (1)
   4 marks
   **Total - 15 marks**

## RIVER BASIN MANAGEMENT

4. (*a*) (i) Possible answers may include:
   Impermeable rock necessary to prevent loss of water through infiltration (1). Hard rock needed in order to support the weight of the dam (1). Ensure that there are no earthquake zones nearby which could destroy the dam (1). Sufficient precipitation to keep the reservoir full (1). Large catchment area to keep the reservoir full (1). Deep valley behind the dam small surface area will reduce loss of water through evaporation (1). Narrow point in the valley to make construction of dam easier (1), and to reduce cost (1).
   *Or any other relevant point.*          4 marks

   (ii) Possible answers may include:
   To reduce the loss of valuable forest areas (1). To prevent the destruction of local people's homes and way of life (1). Building of the dams may result in widespread loss of wildlife (1). Valuable farmland may be lost (1). Destruction of forest may increase global warming (1).
   'Money' must be developed (1).
   *Or any other relevant point.*          4 marks

(*b*) (i) Possible answers may include:
   Improved water supply for people living in a desert area (1). Would reduce the risk of drought (1). Water may be used in agriculture for irrigation (1). Might allow the growing of a greater variety of crops (1). Increased water supply may benefit any industries (1). Water could be used for cooling or as a raw material (1).
   *Or any other relevant point.*          4 marks

(ii) Botswana is likely to object to the loss of its water supply (1). The two countries may not agree as to how much water Namibia should take (1). May result in increased drought in Botswana (1). May reduce living standards in Botswana (1). Okavanga River may have much reduced flow by the time it reaches Botswana (1). *Any other relevant point*.

3 marks

**Total - 15 marks**

## EUROPEAN ENVIRONMENTAL INEQUALITIES

5. (a) (i) *There is no need to refer to individual countries for full marks.*

Highest emissions >5000 metric tonnes from Germany, Czech R, Belgium and UK (1). Between 2500 – 5000 emissions from Poland, Slovakia, Italy (1). Lowest emissions from Northern Europe eg Norway (1) and from Southern Europe eg Spain/Portugal (1).   4 marks

(ii) Areas with large populations emit more air pollution (1), as there are more car fumes (1) and industrial emissions (1). Germany and UK are two highly industrialised countries with many factories emitting gases (1). Areas with high living standards tend to have higher car ownership and more pollution (1). Some less well off areas have less strict air quality control (1)   4 marks

(b) (i) The EU issue legislation to protect river water quality (1). Sewage must be treated (1), companies ignoring legislation can be fined (1), set up cross border co-operation (1), put in place water monitoring stations (1), ban certain chemicals used in agricultural areas (1).

4 marks

(ii) Strategies have had some positive effects on certain rivers eg Rhine where there is less pollution (1), but co-operation is difficult and not all countries agree about costs (1), some industries are still causing pollution (1) and there are still accidental discharges into river (1).

3 marks

**Total = 25 marks**

## DEVELOPMENT AND HEALTH

6. (a) North America uses most energy over 10,000 kg/person (1). Areas using 5000-10000 kg include northern and western Europe (1), Russia (1), Saudi Arabia (1) and Australia/New Zealand (1). The least consumption is in South America or Africa and S.E. Asia (1). Many countries in Africa consume less than 100 kg/person (1) or reference to ELDC/EMDC (1).

(b) *Candidates do not have to mention all six factors to gain full marks.*

Countries with large populations may be able to spend money on improving quality of life (1), they may have to spend money on basics such as food and not on developing industry (1). Countries that are industrialised gain money through exporting products (1), which they can invest in developing roads, schools etc (1). Countries that trade with many partners will gain money (1). Countries that have mainly urban populations tend to be more developed than those with a rural population where wages are low (1). Countries with a good health service have more productive workers (1).

(c) Malaria: found where female anopheles mosquito lives (1) – areas of still water for breeding (1), warm humid conditions (1). Mosquito bites person (1), parasite passed into bloodstream (1), mosquito can also pick up parasite from infected human (1) and then pass it on when it bites someone else (1).

AIDS: unprotected sex (1). Use of infected needles (1). Infection from infected blood transfusions (1). Infection passed on during pregnancy (1). Infected breast milk (1). Lack of education (1). Polygamy (1).

## ENVIRONMENTAL HAZARDS

7. (a) Earth's crust made of plates that move (1). Plates push past each other (1), builds up pressure at plate boundaries (1). Earthquake happens when pressure is released (1). 3 marks

(b) In San Francisco the quake had less effect on landscape as buildings are designed to stand quakes (1), people are prepared for quakes (1), emergency services are quick to respond (1). In Pakistan the houses are not built to stand a quake (1), many people killed under fallen buildings (1), happened in remote area with few emergency services (1), people were not prepared for quake (1).   5 marks

(c) (i) Tropical Storm eg Mitch
Hurricane changed direction frequently so hard to predict landfall (1), warning given to all in Central America so many moved inland (1), but caused jams (1), airforce air lifted people out (1) so saved lives (1).

4 marks

(ii) Government troops helped rescue people (1), Red Cross flew water and blankets (1), USA sent helicopters to take supplies to remote areas (1) and to airlift injured out to hospital (1).   3 marks

**Total = 15 marks**

## INTERMEDIATE 2 GEOGRAPHY 2009

## SECTION A
## PHYSICAL ENVIRONMENTS

**1.** (*a*)  A: Peak District
B: Burren
C: Brecon Beacons                     3 marks

(*b*)  (i)  *Limestone pavement*     903647
*Gorge*                     914638
*Shake hole*                 872662
*Pot holes*                  873647

Mark 4 = 4, 3 = 3, 2 = 2, 1 = 1      4 marks

(ii)  Example: Limestone pavement
Limestone made from decayed remains of skeletons
and sea creatures (1); laid in horizontal layers on sea
bed (1); sedimentary rocks uplifted (1); overlaying rock
removed by glaciation (1); cracks appear as rock dries
out (1); cracks widened into grykes by chemical
weathering (1); limestone dissolved by acid rainwater
(1); clints upstanding blocks (1).
Gorge – Accept river gorge.

*Credit should be given for appropriately annotated
diagrams.*                     4 marks

(iii)  *No marks for grid references.*

*Answers may include:*

It is a low route through a hilly area (1); it passes a
number of attractive tourist features (1)
eg Malham Cove (1); it passes a number of ancient
settlement sites (1); eg hut circles and field systems (1);
services available in Malham (1).

*Or any other valid point.*            4 marks

(*c*)  Mark 2:4, 3:3, 4:2
*Maximum of 5 marks if only one land use mentioned. For full
marks answers must refer to benefits and problems.*

(i)  Economic

For tourism and recreation and leisure visitors spend
more money (1); local people have more jobs (1); local
people therefore have more money to spend (1);
multiplier effect (1); industry/military can also bring in
more money/jobs (1).

Environmental

Tourism/recreation can result in erosion (1); noise
pollution (1); traffic congestion (1); litter (1); military
can limit freedom of people to go where they want (1);
industry can cause visual pollution (1); wildlife habitats
destroyed (1).

*Or any other valid point.*            6 marks

(ii)  Local authorities/NP authorities fined for litter or
dumping (1). NP authorities can fence off eroded areas
(1). Voluntary litter picks in honey pot areas (1).
Council can arrange with military to cease activities on
public holidays (1). National Trust conservation areas
set up (1).

*Or any other valid point.*            4 marks

**Total marks = 25**

## HUMAN ENVIRONMENTS

**2.** (*a*)  (i)  Bigger % males in 20-35 age groups in Urban area (1).
Fewer females in 20-35 groups in Urban area (1).
Bigger % of female in 60+ groups in Rural area (1).
Smaller % of children up to 14 in urban areas (1).

*Credit references to birth and death rates (1).*

*Or any other valid point.*            3 marks

(ii)  Emigration of young males to cities to find work (1).
Women more likely to stay at home to look after family
(1). Return home of some workers to rural area after
living in the city (1). Elderly people staying in the rural
area as did not want to move away (1). Higher birth rate
in rural areas (1). Children can work on farms (1).
Children to look after older parents.        4 marks

(*b*)  EMDCs have child inoculation programme (1). EMDCs
usually have more doctors per head of population (1).
EMDCs have specialist child care maternity units (1).
EMDCs have better access to post natal care (1). EMDCs
have better equipped hospitals (1), better overall standard
of living (1)…etc.                     3 marks

(*c*)  *Mark out of 4 if no named city.*

City councils improving sanitation (1). Installation of clean
water (1). Improving quality of housing (1). Organising
rubbish collection (1). Giving squatters legal ownership of
land (1). Planning new settlements eg Navi Mumbai (1).
Self help schemes (1). Provision of electricity (1).   5 marks

(*d*)  *For full marks both benefits and problems must be mentioned.*

Mark 3:2, 2:3.

Benefits include increased crop yields (1). Better profits for
some farmers (1). Less physical work for people (1).
Problems include fewer jobs for people (1). Expense of
machines (1). Machines need repairs costing more money
(1). Fertilisers increase risk of pollution (1).      5 marks

(*e*)  *For full marks both advantages and disadvantages must be
mentioned.*

Mark 3:2, 2:3.

Plenty of parking space (1). Near to main roads (1). Many
services in one location (1). Reduces congestion in city (1).
Existing shops in CBD suffer (1). Creates extra traffic at
edge of town (1). Uses up Green Belt (1).

*Or any other valid point.*            5 marks

**Total marks = 25**

## SECTION B
## RURAL LAND DEGRADATION

**3.** (*a*)  (i)  There is no rainfall for 5 months (1). For 5 months a
year the soil will be very dry (1); this makes it very
susceptible to wind erosion (1); with little plant growth
in this period, this will increase the risk of soil erosion
(1); when the rains do come in April/May the soil will
be easily washed away (1); will be increased with
intensity of rainfall from June to September (1).

3 marks

(ii)  *Answers should include some detail of methods used, but,
for full marks, should also have some mention of the degree
of effectiveness eg:*

In Niger, tree nurseries were established (1). This has
resulted in afforestation programmes, which has helped
to hold the soil in place (1). People are being educated

about alternative sources of income (1). This has generated additional income (1), which has allowed some groups to send their children to school (1). Better quality breeds of livestock have been introduced (1). People now see the benefits of having smaller numbers of better quality cattle (1).

4 marks

(b) (i) *Answers may include:*

Removal of forest cover exposes soil to heavy rainfall (1); which can wash soil away (1); monoculture can result in loss of soil nutrients (1); Removal of trees means roots no longer able to hold soil in place (1); soil becomes leached (1).

*Accept any other valid point.*  4 marks

(ii) *Answers may include:*

Friends of the Earth persuade people not to buy rainforest products (1); World Bank may refuse funding for development in rainforest areas (1); they could help forest villages to set up tree farms (1); Organisations such as Greenpeace act as pressure groups (1) which try to influence government actions (1); World Wide Fund for Nature takes an active role encouraging public support for the protection of forested areas (1). Local/Government strategies accepted.

4 marks

**Total marks = 15**

## RIVER BASIN MANAGEMENT

4. (a) Rock that is impermeable will store water (1). Areas of high rainfall will have water to store (1). Areas that have many tributary rivers may be better than ones with few (1). Area with narrow V shaped valleys suitable for dam building (1). Large catchment area with plenty of water better suited to development (1).  4 marks

(b) *Answer will depend on river basin chosen eg*

More people now have access to clean water (1). Farmers have regular supply throughout the year (1). Increased crop production (1). Power supply for industry (1). More tourism brings money for local people (1). Power also in more homes (1). Jobs created for some local people (1). Reduced risk of flooding (1).  4 marks

(c) (i) Farmers need water for irrigation (1) or animal needs (1). Tourists look to use water for recreation eg canoeing/speed boating (1). Industry needs water for manufacturing (1) and for power supply (1).  4 marks

(ii) Countries can disagree about water use (1). Countries can pollute a river that then flows into another country (1). Water could be stopped from flowing from one country to another (1). Arguments over who pays for clean up of pollution (1).  3 marks

**Total marks = 15**

## EUROPEAN ENVIRONMENTAL INEQUALITIES

5. (a) *For full marks candidates must refer to both economic and social factors, if not, maximum of 4 marks.*

**Social**: Coastal areas attract large numbers of tourists (1) who drop litter (1) and erode paths and dunelands (1). Sports activities such as jet skiing create noise pollution (1).

**Economic**: Flat coastal areas are prime sites for large industrial development (1) such as steelworks, chemical works or car factories (1). This causes visual pollution (1) and water pollution from heavy metals (1). The transfer of oil by ship can lead to spillages (1). Overfishing can change the marine ecology (1).

*Or any other valid point.*  5 marks

(b) Rivers which flow through industrial regions are more polluted (1) due to industrial waste and chemical spills (1). Rivers in intensive agricultural areas may be polluted by run-off containing chemical fertilizers or pesticides (1). Rivers flowing through large urban areas will be affected by domestic waste and sewage (1).  3 marks

(c) (i) eg coastal areas
The government could encourage tourists to visit inland areas to reduce pressure on coastal regions (1). Money could be provided for new sewage treatment plants (1). More laws and fines for littering (1). Legislation preventing the dumping of industrial waste at sea (1). EU Blue Flag scheme for clean beaches (1).
eg Mountain area
Declare National Park status (1) to control future developments such as quarrying (1). Honeypot strategy to manage busier locations and reduce pressure on other areas (1). Close off eroded areas (1) and re-surface footpaths (1). Educate the public – posters, leaflets – about protecting the environment (1).

*Or any other valid point.*  4 marks

(ii) Candidates must evaluate specific strategies eg the EU Blue Flag Scheme has meant that many beaches are much safer and cleaner (1). New regulations on sewage disposal have improved the quality of Scottish beaches (1). National Park Authorities have more control over new development (1) but conflicts still arise between different interest groups in such areas (1).

*Or any other valid point.*  3 marks

**Total marks = 15**

## DEVELOPMENT AND HEALTH

6. (a) (i) As average income rises, life expectancy increases (1). Countries such as Spain have an average income of $25000 and their life expectancy is over eighty years (1).

Angola has a life expectancy of 41 and its average income is only $1500 (1).

Although Botswana has higher income than Angola its life expectancy is lower (1).  3 marks

(ii) They don't focus on only one aspect of the country (1). They combine both human and economic factors (1) and produce a more realistic picture of a country's well being (1). Single indicators are only averages and don't allow for difference within the country (1) and don't give enough information on the quality of life (1).

4 marks

(b) (i) Heart disease – inability to work (1) and lower life expectancy (1). Increased health costs (1), more hospital beds needed (1). Children can inherit heart disease from parents (1).

Malaria – large numbers of children die at an early age (1), adults unable to work (1), lower productivity (1), limited resources used up on health care (1) hindering development (1).

*Or any other valid point.*  4 marks

(ii) Heart disease – people are now eating a better diet (1), the amount of milk, butter and other fatty products has dropped (1) while the sale of fruit and vegetables has increased (1). The smoking ban has reduced smoking levels (1) and cut down on passive smoking (1). There are more regular check ups (1) and more advanced treatment (1) such as by-pass surgery (1) etc.

Malaria – Drugs are too expensive (1) and the parasite has become resistant to them (1). Insecticides are also expensive (1) and pollute the environment (1). Draining all breeding areas is impractical (1). Bed nets are cheap and quite effective (1). New treatments have been developed which seem to be more effective (1) such as artemesinin/ACT (1). The rate of malaria infection worldwide is still increasing (1).

*Or any other valid point.* 4 marks

**Total marks = 15**

## ENVIRONMENTAL HAZARDS

**7.** (a) In some places the earth's tectonic plates move towards each other (destructive margins) (1) forcing the crust down into the mantle (1) where it melts, rises to the surface and forms a volcano (1). In other places the plates slide slowly past each other (1) releasing sudden bursts of energy (1) which cause earthquakes (1). 3 marks

(b) (i) Volcanic eruptions – monitor seismic activity (1), watch for changes in gas levels (1) bulges in the mountainside (1) or unusual wildlife behaviour (1).

Earthquakes – use laser equipment to detect land movement (1). Sound equipment to detect tremors (1). Examine previous patterns of earthquake activity (1).

Mark 1:3, 2:2 or 3:1 3 marks

(ii) Short term – emergency medical for those injured (1) tents and blankets to provide shelter (1) bottled water as supplies will be cut off (1) moving equipment and sniffer dogs to locate those trapped in fallen buildings (1).

Long term – Money needed to repair infrastructure (1) eg roads, electricity supplies, water systems (1).

*Or any other valid point.* 4 marks

(c) *No reference to a specific tropical storm – mark out of four.*

Tropical storms cause widespread flooding (1) and destroy farmland (1). Trees are knocked over (1) and heavy rain washes away soil (1). Many people are made homeless (1). Power lines, bridges and roads are destroyed (1). Water and sewage problems cause outbreaks of disease (1). Economic development is badly affected (1) and national debt increases due to the cost of repairs (1).

*For full marks effects on landscape and people must be mentioned.* 5 marks

**Total marks = 15**

## INTERMEDIATE 2 GEOGRAPHY 2010

## SECTION A
## PHYSICAL ENVIRONMENTS

**1.** (a) A: Loch Lomond and/or Trossachs
B: River Tay
C: Buchan (accept N.E. Scotland) N.E. Coast, Moray Coast
*3 × 1 mark* 3 marks

(b) (i) Truncated spur 135057
Arête 206068
Corrie 159103
Hanging valley 183097
*4 × 1 mark* 4 marks

(ii) As the glacier moves down the valley (1) it deepens and widens the valley (1) by plucking and abrasion (1). Terminal moraine may be deposited at the end of the glacier (1). This moraine prevents water from draining away, forming a ribbon lake (1).
*For full marks, formation of the lake must be mentioned. If not out of 3.* 4 marks
*Credit should be given for annotated diagrams. (3) for V-shaped valley.*

(c) *For full marks candidates must describe the river and its valley, otherwise mark out of three.*
The River Calder at 064103 is narrow/straight (1) and fast flowing (1) in a southerly direction (1) through a steep sided V-shaped valley (1). It is joined by a tributary (Worm Gill) at 066090 (1). The river then flows south west (1) and becomes wider (1). It meanders slightly (1) over a narrow flood plain (1). The river has two islands/eyots (1) in 0608 (1). The valley becomes wider (1) and its side less steep (1) as it approaches Calder Bridge.
*Or any other valid point.* 4 marks

(d) Eg tourism causes problems with increased litter (1), traffic congestion at peak periods (1), footpath erosion in popular walking areas (1).
Farming activities are often in conflict with walker's rights of access (1) walkers leaving gates open (1), dogs chasing sheep (1), stone walls damaged (1), etc.
Industry/quarrying creates air and noise pollution (1), heavy traffic on narrow roads (1) and spoils the appearance of the scenery (1).
Commercial forestry is unpopular as it looks unnatural (1) and may restrict access for walkers (1).
*Or any other valid point.* 6 marks

(e) Planning permission for developments which may cause conflict can be refused in National Park areas (1). Different recreational activities may be zoned (1) such as waterskiing and sailing (1). Park rangers are employed to prevent problems developing (1). Visitor centre staff aim to educate the public about the "Countryside Code/Outdoor Access Code" (1). One-way systems, pedestrianised areas (1) and improved public transport (1) are introduced to reduce the effect of traffic congestion (1). Voluntary bodies such as the National Trust protect areas by buying land and buildings (1), maintaining walls and footpaths (1), and protecting important wildlife habitats (1).
*Or any other valid point.* 4 marks

**Total marks = 25**

## HUMAN ENVIRONMENTS

**2.** (a) (i) In 1950 population growth rate was approx 1.7% (1), it then went up to 2%, in 1960s and 70s (1), it then fell from 70s to 80s (1), then steadied during 80s (1) but since

then has fallen (1) and is projected to fall further (1).
  3 marks

(ii) *If no difference mentioned maximum 5 marks. 1 mark for difference – population growth in EMDC hardly changing whereas in ELDCs rapid growth.*
EMDCs are predicted to hardly change, this is because of increased use of family planning (1), less desire for large families (1), later marriages for women (1). ELDCs are continuing to grow due to need for families to look after elderly (1), bring in money for family (1), lack of education on family planning (1).
*Or any other valid point.*  6 marks

(b) *Maximum 1 mark for explanation.*
Kenya – majority of the population are under the age of 15 (1), population numbers decrease as age increases (1), smaller numbers of people found over 60 (1). Nearly 7% under 4 years of age (1). Low life expectancy (1) high degree of juvenility (1) older males living longer than females (1). Italy – largest number of people are in the economically active ages (1), fewer young people under 19 (1), more women then men (1), increased numbers of elderly population (1). % of young people drops dramatically (1).
*Or any other valid point.*  4 marks

(c) Examples may come from ELDCs and/or EMDCs.
Some farmland is lost to new housing developments (1). There is increased traffic on the roads during peak times (1). Commuter villages grow in size (1) and there is often an increase in house prices in rural areas (1). Young people from the rural area move away as they cannot afford the houses (1). Some local services are lost as urban commuters do not use them (1). Wildlife pushed further back into rural areas (1). Pollution (1).
*Or any other valid point.*  4 marks

(d) Indian farmers started to use HYV of rice (1). Farmers are using more fertilisers to help crops (1). Machinery has increased efficiency (1). Land reform has made bigger farms (1).
*Or any other valid point.*  4 marks

(e) Labour is cheaper (1) which reduces overall costs of product manufacture (1). Workforce is motivated (1). There are fewer industrial disputes (1). Transport infrastructure is very good (1). Government will help with initial set up costs (1). Close to large markets eg China or India (1).
*Or any other valid point.*  4 marks
  **Total marks = 25**

# SECTION B
## RURAL LAND DEGRADATION

3. (a) (i) 1 mark for comparing statements: maximum 1 mark for %.
The Philippines has lost the greatest amount of its forest cover (1), 32% (1). Indonesia, Nepal and Cambodia have lost 20% or more (1). Vietnam has increased its forest cover by the largest amount (1), 38% (1). China and India have also increased their forest cover (1) etc.  4 marks

(ii) Large areas have been cleared by timber companies (1) and hardwood is sold to other countries (1). Forest has been cleared for settlement (1) and new farmland (1) due to expanding population (1) and to increase food production (1). Forest is also destroyed due to mineral extraction (1).
*Or any other valid point.*  4 marks

(b) *Mark 3:1; 2:2 or 1:3*
Physical – drought conditions cause vegetation to die (1) and soil to dry up (1). Dry soil is blown away by high winds (1) as there are no roots to bind the soil (1). Seasonal rains can also

wash away fragile soil (1) causing gullying (1). Human – overpopulation puts pressure on farmland (1). Trees are cut down for firewood (1) and to make new farmland (1). Overgrazing damages the vegetation (1). Monoculture weakens soil structure (1) making it less fertile (1).
*Or any other valid point.*  4 marks

(c) Strategies include: contour ploughing (1) and stone lines (1) to reduce runoff (1), crop rotation (1), planting dune areas with drought resistant species (1), fencing off overgrazed areas (1), reafforestation (1).
*Or any other valid point.*  3 marks
  **Total marks = 15**

## RIVER BASIN MANAGEMENT

4. (a) The rock type can affect water storage (1). Permeable rock is not suitable as water will drain away (1). Impermeable rock will hold water and prevents seepage (1). Steep sided valleys are good to help dam construction (1). Areas with high rainfall will provide adequate water supply (1).
*Descriptive and explanatory points acceptable.*
*Or any other valid point.*  4 marks

(b) Answer will vary depending on project chosen.
(i) Project was needed to help prevent flooding (1). Dam provided HEP (1). Irrigation water was available (1). River was controlled (1).
  4 marks

(ii) Local people lost homes (1). Local wildlife was endangered (1). Increase in disease in some places (1). Loss of fishing (1).
*Or any other valid point.*  3 marks

(c) *Both economic and social must be mentioned for full marks.*
**Economic** – increased power for industry (1). Industry attracted to area (1) and jobs created (1). Improved river navigation (1).
**Social** – electricity for housing (1). Improved water supply (1). Improved amenities for local people – due to tourism/more shops/services (1). Jobs created (1).
*Or any other valid point.*  4 marks
  **Total marks = 15**

## EUROPEAN ENVIRONMENTAL INEQUALITIES

5. (a) (i) Most of the rivers flow to the north and west (1); one flows to the east (1); two flow into the North Sea (1); one flows into the English Channel (1); one flows into the Bay of Biscay (1); two flow into the Atlantic Ocean (1); three flow into the Baltic Sea (1); one flows into the Black Sea (1).
*Any general description is acceptable as is reference to areas with very few rivers.*
*Or any other valid point.*  3 marks

(ii) *5 marks for other farming or industry.*
Farming can wash fertilisers and pesticides (1) into rivers. Industrial waste can be pumped into rivers (1). Fall-out from air pollution can also enter rivers (1). Discharge from oil industry/ pipeline etc (1). Chemical dumping (1).
*Or any other valid point.*  5 marks

(b) (i) Stricter controls on factory emissions (1); fines for companies which break rules (1); reducing the use of cars (1); encourage car sharing (1); improved public transport services (1); improve the efficiency of vehicle engines (1); discourage single use of cars (1); air filters on industrial chimneys (1); use of catalytic converters (1); congestion charges (1); reduction of $SO_2$ emissions (1); reduction of coal and oil fired power stations (1).
*Or any other valid point.*  4 marks

(ii) Park and ride systems around cities have met with some success (1); too many people still enjoy the use of their own car (1); more people using bicycles (1).
*Or any other valid point.* 3 marks
**Total marks = 15**

## DEVELOPMENT AND HEALTH

**6.** (*a*) Climate –

certain climates can limit development of a country eg hot dry climates (1); cold climates (1); high humidity (1).

Relief –

development encouraged with low-lying flat land (1); high altitude can make development difficult (1); mountainous areas can make transport difficult (1).

Resources –

countries with plenty of resources can develop industrially (1); they can also make money from trading (1).

Environment –

rainforest (1), hot desert (1) or cold desert areas will be difficult to develop (1). Development is easier in temperate areas (1).

Natural Disasters –

countries not liable to natural disasters will be easier to develop (1) natural disasters cost countries money to re-build (1).

*More than one physical factor should be mentioned for full marks.* 4 marks

(*b*) (i) Biggest problem in southern Africa (1); Central Africa also a significant problem (1); Eastern Europe (1); and Russia (1); also in south-east Asia (1). 4 marks

(ii) **AIDS –**

introduction of health education programmes (1); compulsory testing of people (1); increase the availability of ARV drugs to treat the disease (1); distribution of free condoms (1); use of radio and TV to get the message over (1).

**Heart Disease –**

increased funding of research into the disease (1); encourage people to eat more healthily (1); encourage people to take more exercise (1); stop-smoking campaigns (1); educate people on how to reduce stress levels (1); encourage people to have regular check-ups (1) for cholesterol (1) and blood pressure (1); increased use of technology eg pacemakers (1); drugs (1).

*Or any other valid point.* 4 marks

(iii) **AIDS –**

drugs available but not enough trained staff in developing countries (1); many isolated areas which are difficult to reach (1); many people not aware they have the disease (1); testing facilities poor (1); some people try to avoid being tested (1); some drugs too expensive (1); education campaigns difficult due to illiteracy (1) and different dialects and languages (1).

**Heart Disease –**

evidence that better diet is working (1); decrease in consumption of butter and full milk (1); people are eating more fruit (1); evidence that people are still not taking enough exercise (1); numbers smoking has now decreased (1); no evidence that stress levels are decreasing (1); people appear to be getting more regular check-ups (1).

*Or any other valid point.* 3 marks
**Total marks = 15**

## ENVIRONMENTAL HAZARDS

**7.** (*a*) Track SE to NW (1), crossing the Tropic of Cancer (1) heading toward SE USA (1), *or any other valid point.*
3 marks

(*b*) *Credit annotated diagram.*
Sea temperatures must be over 27°C (1); low atmospheric pressure (1); spiralling winds (1); large expanse of water is needed (1); rising air (1). Location between tropics (1).
4 marks

(*c*) (i) *Landscape and population must be mentioned for full marks.*
Buildings destroyed (1); villages cut off (1); lines of communication destroyed (1); landslides (1); fires may break out (1); severed water pipes (1).
People killed/injured (1); people buried alive (1); outbreak of disease (1)
*Or any other valid point.* 4 marks

(ii) Better building techniques (1); improved methods of prediction (1); monitoring of active earthquake zones (1); use of tiltmeters to measure Earth movements (1); practising earthquake drills (1); improved preparation of emergency services (1).
*Or any other valid point.* 4 marks
**Total marks = 15**

# INTERMEDIATE 2 GEOGRAPHY 2011

## SECTION A
## PHYSICAL ENVIRONMENTS

**1.** (*a*)  (i) Thames
(ii) Cairngorms/Grampian Mountains
(iii) The Burren                                    3 marks

(*b*) Headlands and bays are most likely to be found in areas where there are bands of alternating soft and hard rock which meet the coast at right angles; the softer rock, for example clay will erode more quickly forming bays which may have sandy beaches; whilst the harder rock, for example chalk will erode more slowly forming headlands which jut out into the sea.
*Or any other valid point. Credit should be given for appropriate annotated diagrams.*            4 marks

(*c*)  (i) A   A4139
B   Railway
C   Cycle Path
D   Forestry                               4 marks

(ii) The route is easily accessible by road and there are many car parks for parking; there are many features of scenic interest along the route for example cliffs; there are also features of historic interest such as castles; camp sites along the route provide a place for walkers to stay and there are services within the settlements for walkers to rest and eat; the area is part of a national park and so will have many landscape features, vegetation and animals of interest.
*Or any other valid point. Maximum of 1 mark for grid references.*                                 4 marks

(*d*) *For full marks the candidate must refer to both environmental and economic impact.*

(i) **Leisure and recreation**

**Economic**

Visitors to the area for recreational purposes may hire equipment such as skis in the local area. This brings money to the local economy and provides jobs for local people, although these are likely to be seasonal in the case of winter sports; it is likely that recreational visitors such as those for winter sports will spend a few days in the area and therefore require accommodation in the local area; many services will be provided for recreational visitors, for example specialist equipment shops but this may be at the expense of services for local residents. Goods sold in these shops may also be at higher prices.

**Environmental**

Recreational visitors may cause footpath erosion in upland areas and also those undertaking winter sports create scars on the landscape as vegetation and soil is trampled during the winter season. Equipment erected for winter sports is unsightly eg chairlifts; recreational visitors may drop litter in the upland area which is unsightly and can cause harm to animals; they may also leave farmers' gates open which can cause animals to escape from fields; walkers' dogs may worry sheep; visitors using the area for recreation may park their cars at the side of the road causing erosion to the grass verges and also traffic congestion on narrow country roads.
*Or any other valid point.*                    6 marks

(ii) *For example, industry stone extraction*
Quarries and cement works can be filled in and landscaped once they have closed. Vegetation and trees can be used to shield the quarry from view; quarries can be turned into water features and these can be used for recreational purposes; levy schemes have been introduced to reduce the impact on communities; these include the provision of safe play areas and insulation and double glazing for local housing; government money has been given to organisations such as English Heritage to repair monuments etc which have been damaged by stone extraction; environmentally friendly methods of transportation such as nets on lorries are also used. Industrial buildings are made from local materials and are low level helping them to blend in with the surrounding landscape.
*Or any other valid point.*                    4 marks
                                        **Total = 25 marks**

## HUMAN ENVIRONMENTS

**2.** (*a*) Some areas may be too steeply sloping for building on. In some areas there may be fertile soils which allows people to grow enough food to feed themselves. Some areas may be too high for people to live comfortably. Temperate climate would make for a suitable place to live. Lack of water may prevent people from living in certain areas. High humidity could be a problem. Other areas may be too cold. Areas with many natural resources are usually attractive places for people to live.
Areas with good transport links usually attract people; such areas usually attract industry, thus giving employment opportunities. Remote/isolated areas do not usually attract many people.
*Or any other valid point.*
*Both physical and human factors must be mentioned for full marks.*                                   5 marks

(*b*) Few children are being born which could result in a shortage of working adults in years to come. This will result in fewer people paying tax which could affect the nation's economy. Jobs could be lost in nurseries, schools etc. The country will start to develop an ageing population. More money will need to be spent on pensions. The cost of health care for the elderly will rise. More demand for care services such as meals on wheels. More demand for sheltered housing and old people's homes.
*Or any other valid point.*                    5 marks

(*c*) Cost of car parking has been made very expensive. In some cases there is now no free parking. Some cities have introduced congestion charges. A lot of investment has been put into public transport systems. Fares have been reduced in order to encourage greater use by the public. Bus lanes have been introduced to try to speed up the service. Some cities have invested heavily in underground rail systems.
*Or any other valid point.*
*For full marks there must be some sort of statement indicating the success of the methods.*          6 marks

(*d*) **Benefits**
Increase in local employment. Local farming and fishing has benefitted from an increased market. Local handicraft industries have also benefitted. An increase in money going into the economy. Local people can therefore benefit from improved provision of services.

**Problems**

Farming has lost land to tourist development. Fishermen have lost coastal sites to hotels. Traditional village occupations are decreasing. Water shortages can be a problem. Beaches can become contaminated with sewage. Local wildlife could be under threat.
*Or any other valid point.*
*Both benefits and problems must be mentioned.*  5 marks

(e) Visual appearance of the environment has improved; spoil heaps have been removed or landscaped; tall chimneys have been removed. Waterways and rivers have been cleaned up. There has been a reduction in air pollution and noise pollution. New industrial areas are usually landscaped with gardens, trees and water.
*Or any other valid point.*  4 marks

**Total = 25 marks**

## SECTION B
## RURAL LAND DEGRADATION

3. (a) Overgrazing in an area can leave the soil vulnerable to soil erosion as the lack of vegetation no longer provides protection for the soil. If the rains fail then sufficient vegetation doesn't grow and this can lead to overgrazing. The animals also compact the soil by trampling which reduces the amount of infiltration and so increase soil run off and erosion. This results in nomads farming marginal areas leading to land degradation. As arable farmers are forced to increase yields for growing populations there is less fallow time (resting time for soils) which reduces the amount of nutrients in the soil. With unreliable rainfall crops fail and the soil becomes susceptible to erosion and degradation.
*Or any other valid point.*  6 marks

(b) (i) Deforestation can lead to the loss of resources from the forest, for example the loss of hardwood timber, rare plants, animals, birds and insects. Animal and plant habitats will be lost and this could damage the ecosystem of the rainforest. The loss of plants could jeopardise future possible cures for diseases such as cancer. The native peoples of the rainforest will be displaced from their homes and may end up living in reserves or forced out of the rainforest altogether. Indigenous people could also fall ill from diseases and infections brought in by the fellers, this could lead to death. Traditional customs and cultures could be lost.
*Or any other valid point.*  5 marks

(ii) The consequence of deforestation can be reduced in many ways. For example, selective tree felling allows only trees which have matured fully to be cut down. This means that rather than a whole area being felled only single trees are felled and so young trees survive. Afforestation of areas which have been felled helps to replace trees which have been cut down. Reservations have been created in protected areas of forest, tree felling is banned and these provide a safe place for native peoples to live. Crops can be grown amongst forested areas to prevent soil erosion through clear felling for agriculture this is known as agroforestry. Fines can be placed on those who fell areas which are protected and education helps to make people aware of the consequences of clear felling.
*Or any other valid point.*  4 marks

**Total = 15 marks**

## RIVER BASIN MANAGEMENT

4. (a) Water is evaporated from the sea. Condensation takes place turning the water vapour into clouds. Winds blow clouds inland towards the mountains. Here, they are forced to rise causing further condensation which results in precipitation. Some of this water is stored in the mountains as snow and ice. Water flows into streams to make its way back to the sea. Some infiltration into the ground; this may result in some underground flow back to the sea. Some water may be stored in the vegetation which may lead to transpiration from trees through their leaves. Some water may also be stored in inland lakes. There may be some evaporation from these lakes.
*Or any other valid point.*  5 marks

(b) Impermeable rock could increase the amount of water which can be stored as very little would be lost through seepage; steep ground could increase surface run-off. Lack of vegetation cover would increase surface run-off. Forested areas would increase the amount of water which would be stored. A large drainage basin would obviously increase the amount of water which could be stored. Areas with high rainfall have more water in the river basin.
*Or any other valid point.*  5 marks

(c) Possible answers may include:
Large forested areas may have been flooded or cut down. Animal habitats may be destroyed. Rare plant or animal species may be endangered. Less water may now reach the river estuary; this could affect the number of fish in the river. Particularly fragile areas eg caves may be destroyed.
*Or any other valid point.*  5 marks

**Total = 15 marks**

## EUROPEAN ENVIRONMENTAL INEQUALITIES

5. (a) Northern Italy has high air pollution as major industrial centres here. Coastal areas have moderate pollution as lower population density. Low air pollution in southern toe of Italy with low population density. Alps block polluted air. Moderate density at large cities.
*Or any other relevant point.*  4 marks

(b) *For full marks at least two of the factors must be mentioned.*
Areas with dense population produce more rubbish. Transport like ships can spill oil or discharge materials into the sea. Areas with high living standards will clean up pollution and not discharge sewage into the sea. Areas with lots of industrial activity near the coast can pollute it.
*Or any other relevant point.*  5 marks

(c) Some candidates may answer both (i) and (ii) together.
Mark 4:2, 2:4 or 3:3

(i) Councils can fine polluters. River clean ups organised by volunteers. Monitoring river pollution. Joint control schemes where river runs through different countries. EU introduced laws on environment.

(ii) Many rivers now cleaner. EU regulations have helped improve quality control. Some rivers still receive pollution. Difficulty of political agreement where river crosses several countries.
*Or any other relevant point.*  6 marks

**Total = 15 marks**

# DEVELOPMENT AND HEALTH

**6.** (*a*) Countries with an educated workforce make more money. Countries with a good health service are more developed as less money drained from economy. Countries with many industries have more people in employment and generate more wealth.

Countries with difficult climates can find development hindered. Countries with limited natural resources have less money to spend on development.
*Or any other relevant point.*                     6 marks

(*b*) Aids – sharing dirty needles, unprotected sex with infected person, babies drinking breast milk of infected mother, sharing body fluids, infected blood transfusions.
Heart disease – lack of exercise, overeating/drinking, lifestyle/stress, hereditary, eating foods high in fat.
                                                   4 marks

(*c*) Loss of workforce. Hinders development leading to fewer jobs. Costs of hospital treatment increase. Less wealth in country. Death rate increases. Emotional impact on relatives and friends. Loss of tourist revenue.
*Or any other relevant point.*                     5 marks
                                         **Total = 15 marks**

# ENVIRONMENTAL HAZARDS

**7.** (*a*) Plates move apart and magma can come up. Plates moving under each other can cause friction which results in liquid rock being forced up. Credit explanations of destructive and constructive boundaries.
                                                   5 marks

(*b*) Methods will include laser monitoring, motion detectors, scientists monitoring, gas analysis, information from previous events, animal movements.
*Or any other relevant point.*                     4 marks

(*c*) Both types of aid must be mentioned for full marks.
Mark 3:3, 4:2 or 2:4

Long term may include:
Roads will need rebuilt after being washed away to help transport improve, flood prevention measures put in place to help control future events, evacuation procedures improved.

Short term may include:
Shelter for homeless, food and water, medical aid for injured, voluntary workers.
*Or any other relevant point.*                     6 marks
                                         **Total 15 marks**

Hey! I've done it

Published by Bright Red Publishing Ltd, 6 Stafford Street, Edinburgh, EH3 7AU
Tel: 0131 220 5804, Fax: 0131 220 6710, enquiries: sales@brightredpublishing.co.uk,
www.brightredpublishing.co.uk

Official SQA answers to 978-1-84948-199-1
2007-2011